Cab Forward 4294

Southern Pacific Railroad's Signature Locomotive

David N. Anderson, Vincent C. Cipolla,
& Russell M.H. O'Day

Cab Forward 4294

Southern Pacific Railroad's Signature Locomotive

David N. Anderson, Vincent C. Cipolla, & Russell M.H. O'Day

Cab-forward No. 4294 is located at the
California State Railroad Museum
125 "I" Street Sacramento, CA 95814

Museum Information/Front Desk 916-323-9280

Dedicated to Bob Church, a true gentleman and winner of the Gerald M. Best Senior Achievement Award presented by the Railway and Locomotive Historical Society for contributions to railroad history. Bob's best-known book is ***Cab Forward*** and he has written a number of other exceptional books related to the Southern Pacific, especially its steam locomotives.

Want to learn More? Join the Southern Pacific Historical & Technical Society; for details see their website at: **sphts.org**

Acknowledgments

The authors wish to thank the following CSRM docents, editor, and graphic artist were involved in the preparation of a document that preceded this book: Gerald Rood (document preparation), Milo Hewit (photographer), Judy Fischette (editing), Julia Owens (graphic artist), and Russell M.H. O'Day (research and writing). Cab forward roster courtesy of CSRM Docent Marvin Schurke. Introduction written by Docent Scott Inman. All photographs by Milo Hewit unless noted.

The cover photograph features Extra 4294 with a train of refrigerator cars westbound near Burbank, California in 1948. Hal Jackson photo.

Books for enthusiasts by enthusiasts

www.aeronautbooks.com

ISBN: 978-1-935881-99-5

Design and layout: Jack Herris
Cover design: Aaron Weaver & Jack Herris
Digital photo editing: Aaron Weaver & Jack Herris

Table of Contents

X4294
X4294
4294
4294
4294
SP

1: 4294 at Work

Above: Builder's photo of SP 4294 ready to leave the factory in Philadelphia, PA, in February 1944. Note the white trim on the drivers and running boards applied for this photograph. Paul Koehler collection

Above: SP 4294 in pre-1946 markings. Will Whittaker collection

Facing Page: SP 4294 on display in the CSRM. Boyd Reyes photo

Above: SP 4294 pulling the 4th section of a reefer block X4294 at Roseville, Feb. 20, 1946. Francis Smith Photo

Above: SP 4294 pulled an extra reefer block SP westbound near Burbank in 1948. The lower front of the cab is now painted silver to make the locomotive easier to see as a safety measure. Silver paint on this manner on cab forwards and silver on the front of smoke boxes on other steam locomotives was standardized in mid 1946. Hal Jackson photo

Above: SP 4294 at Taylor Yard in Los Angeles, January 2, 1950. Gerald M. Best photo

Above: SP 4294 in service and ready for her next call. Malcom Gaddis photo, SPH&TS Collection

Above: SP 4294 at Colton, January 23, 1950. Lew Harris photo

Below: SP 4294 serving as a mid-train helper. Malcom Gaddis photo, SPH&TS Collection

Above: SP 4294 at Watsonville Junction, April 23, 1955. Paul Koehler collection

Above: SP 4294 in storage in Sacramento in 1974. Don Ball photo

Above: Cab-forwards fill the Roseville roundhouse in 1937 for a publicity photo. Scott Inman Collection

Above: A cab-forward undergoing service in Oakland, September 11, 1956. Gordon Glattenberg photo

2: Introduction by Scott Inman

Above: In 1948, SP Extra 4294 leads a westbound reefer block over Beaumont Hill on the Los Angeles Division. The AC-12 class represented the pinnacle of steam locomotive design on the Southern Pacific. Hal Jackson Photo

Many major railroads of the 20th century featured trademarks of machinery and power, symbolized by their signature locomotives. More than a slogan or even a premier passenger train, a locomotive fleet had the ability to captivate the public, and the Southern Pacific Railroad was not immune. The magnificent technological landmark of engineering capability employed by the SP established this trademark. In total, 256 cab-in-fronts, or "Malleys" were utilized by Southern Pacific as one of the largest fleets of articulated steam locomotives ever assembled. The last example of this technology pioneered by the Southern Pacific Railroad survives today in Sacramento at the California State Railroad Museum. Nearly 600,000 school children and visitors each year awe in amazement of the size, weight, design, and majesty of what today is fittingly the largest steam locomotive in California. Southern Pacific 4294 is the last of its kind in existence in the world, and was the final cab forward produced for the railroad by the Baldwin Locomotive Works following 35 years of mechanical engineering and design advancements. The railroad's challenging need for ever expanding power, reliability, and tractive effort led to the locomotive represented in this guide.

Southern Pacific was the only major railroad in America to utilize steam technology with the cab and firebox in the front of the locomotive. This concept, however, originated a decade before SP ordered the first of their cab-in-front types. The original design for this radical concept was a joint effort between Master Mechanic William Thomas and General Superintendent Thomas Stetson of the North Pacific Coast Railroad. In 1900, the two mechanical engineers combined efforts and built NPC No. 21, originally to be named "Thomas Stetson" for the railroad's senior manager. The patent for this concept applied to the watertube boiler in combination with the cab-in-front design, rather than the positioning of the engine and tender. Even though the engine was only in service a year or two before being condemned after a low-water incident, this would later allow Southern Pacific and Baldwin an opportunity to implement the design on a larger scale.

The first articulated locomotives ordered by the Southern Pacific arrived in 1909 and were delivered to the Sacramento Division for use over Donner Pass. The two original Baldwin engines were No. 4000–4001, and classified as type MC-1. MC was the abbreviation for Mallet Consolidation because these engines were both compound and featured eight driving wheels per engine. Upon delivery, they both performed to expectations in mountain territory where grades up to 2.4% were

Above: North Pacific Coast No. 21 was in many ways the prototype for what became Southern Pacific's fleet of 256 cab-in-front locomotives. Pacific Coast Chapter, R&LHS Roy Graves Collection

continuous. The trial runs for these machines were performed by Engineer W.H. Kopka and Fireman F.E. Keenan, who tried their best to pace the engines for faults in tracking abilities and firing quality. After having serious doubts the engine could be kept hot as oil burners, their fears quickly subsided when the locomotives exceeded expectations.

Upon the delivery of the new Mallets, the Mountain Subdivision of the Sacramento Division had approximately 40 miles of wooden snow sheds covering the main track, and 39 tunnels. Enter the negative effects of exhaust, steam, heat, and deafening noise. With the increase in power for these locomotives came a huge challenge of crew asphyxiation caused by the gasses of the exhaust ahead of the crew inside the cab. With smaller engines, exhaust was less plentiful and generally cooler. The new MC-1 engines required heavy firing to keep the steam pressure, and with that came a powerful combination of steam and oil smoke wickedly belching from the stack with every chuff of the cylinders.

After experimenting with ventilation systems and masks, the only remedy that proved successful was to run the locomotives

Above: Southern Pacific's first Mallet Consolidation was C.P. 4000 built in 1909. This builder's photo shows what the engine looked like at the Baldwin Locomotive Works Philadelphia Plant when it was built. The gray primer on the boiler was only for purposes of the construction photo and would be painted over with black before shipment to the railroad. Scott Inman Collection

Above: Freshly delivered from Baldwin Locomotive Works, Southern Pacific's first cab-ahead posed at the Sacramento Shops in February 1910. This was undoubtedly for testing and crew orientation. Chalk markings on the cab face indicate notes from the mechanical department. Of note are the early oil-fueled lighting appliances including the headlight, indicators, and class lights. Scott Inman Collection

in reverse, so the exhaust was behind the crew. This presented several logistical challenges, because the engineer was on the wrong side of the track to see signals and capture train orders. Additionally, the Mallets did not track well when shoving their tenders in front of the cab. Following the experimental runs, a meeting was held in Sacramento at the office of Superintendent of Motive Power Taylor W. Heintzelman. Other attendees included Road Foreman of Engines D.H. Blair, General Air Brake Inspector H.H. Forney, Chief Draftsman F.E. Russell Sr., Chief Chemist Charles Browning Jr., and Chemist B.F. Kline. Because the locomotives operated efficiently, but were not a success in operation, the meeting's tone was bleak until Mr. Browning spoke of NPC No. 21's brief career as a narrow gauge cab-in-front. Browning argued this design could be adapted to solve the Mallet problem, and urged Frank Russell with the cooperation of Chief Mechanical Engineer Howard Stillman in San Francisco to work out the details for conversion. Upon initial contact with Stillman, there was great skepticism for Russell and the committee's idea of a cab-ahead Mallet design. It had not been too many years since the innovative Master Mechanic at Sacramento, A.J. Stevens, and his debacle of Central Pacific's 4-10-0 "El Gobernador" which turned out to be an abysmal failure and relegated to helper service. Despite their concerns, they began working on the blueprints for a reverse pattern engine.

Some previously published works have claimed Baldwin proposed the original cab-ahead recommendation to Southern Pacific, when in fact the company's engineering department in San Francisco supplied the information, and Baldwin then adapted conventional locomotives under construction at that time. The first cab-aheads delivered to SP in February and March 1910 were 15 class MC-2 locomotives numbered 4002–4016. They were received with shock, dismay, and curiosity by crews and shop forces. Some enginemen refused crew calls because they felt the machines were "death traps!" Soon, however, the benefits demonstrated were seen to outweigh any risk and the unobstructed view of the main track ahead of the train was welcomed.

Southern Pacific became very enamored with the MC class and decided to order a passenger version of the cab-ahead for delivery in 1911. Originally built as 2-6-6-2 types, the 12 engines were class MM-2, or Mallet Mogul due to their six driving wheels per engine. These were the original 4200 class and quickly were more troubled than their larger counterparts. The greatest problem with the MM-2 design was the overall short wheelbase that created excessive lateral motion and hunting at speed. This also caused the overhang of the cab on curves to be so severe that corner posts on the cabs were frequently torn off in snow sheds. The poor handling created additional issues such as excessive flange wear on the lead driver

Above: The original modern cab-ahead, AC-4 No. 4100 paused at Lathrop California on May 22, 1952 with a nine-car excursion special chartered by the Pacific Coast Chapter, Railway and Locomotive Historical Society. The AC-4 class featured modern appliances and design methods, while mostly retaining a traditional appearance. Scott Inman Collection

of the No. 2 engine and frequent derailments caused by the lead pony truck jumping the rails. Following a bad accident with MM-2 No. 4208 on the point of SP's premier passenger train, the "Overland Limited," the entire class was removed from service and taken to Sacramento for rebuilding. They emerged from the shops in 1914 with a modified frame and a new wheel arrangement of type 4-6-6-2. This new MM design provided better tracking and reliability, eliminating all issues from the factory. Despite their success following rebuilding, they only remained in passenger service a few more years due to their 63 inch driver diameter and resulting slow speed.

SP would go on to buy additional Mallet classes such as 12 MC-4s in 1911 and 20 MC-6s in 1912–13, all of the 2-8-8-2 variety. This roster would fulfill the cab-ahead fleet for many years until 1923, when the decision was made to rebuild the original conventional MC-1 class into cab-aheads. Nos. 4000 and 4001 were taken to Sacramento and out-shopped in 1923. The late 1920s and 1930s saw most of the earlier Mallet-type compound locomotives rebuilt to simple steam to reduce maintenance and enable higher speed. Several reasons for this included the low-speed bottlenecks developing on Donner Pass, better performance in drag freight service in uphill territory, and stiffening competition from trucks demanding higher speed with the same tractive effort. A paradox of this progress was the fact that this same technology which enabled the cab-ahead locomotives eventually limited their capabilities.

With double tracking and modern signaling complete on Donner Pass in 1924, Southern Pacific decided their 15-year hiatus of new cab-ahead purchases would be coming to an end. The result was the "modern cab-ahead" delivered from Baldwin as a simple locomotive. As a trial following the rebuilding of compound engines, SP General Superintendent of Motive Power George McCormick negotiated with Baldwin to deliver 10 new AC-4 type engines in the fall of 1928. These were classified as Articulated Consolidations, because they were no longer Mallet compounds, even though crews would refer to them as "Malleys" until the end of steam. They were purchased with dual freight and passenger service in mind, but they primarily worked freight between Roseville and Sparks. AC-4s were so successful that SP ordered 16 class AC-5s and 25 class AC-6s. Each class became larger and heavier, with the new ACs featuring many design upgrades such as a conical-type boiler, larger firebox, and two-section smokebox. The tenders of these locomotives were 16,000 gallon semi-cylindrical Commonwealth waterbottom-type with six-wheel trucks. They had a capacity of 4,860 gallons of oil, but were never filled to capacity because of the pressurized compartment to move the fuel the distance required to reach the firing injectors.

The AC-6 class truly represented a shift in technology from the AC-4/5 and future classes. Their boiler pressure increased from 235 to 250 psi and they had a higher cutoff rate, bumping their tractive effort to 123,400 pounds (10,460 pounds higher than the previous 4-8-8-2s). Bar-type throttles in the cabs were replaced by the swinging style. SP competitor Western Pacific was so impressed with the new designs, their motive power department seriously considered ordering their first cab-aheads, but bought 2-8-8-2 Mallets after polling crews.

The next wave of 25 Malleys were delivered between

Above: Fitted with test instruments such as a doghouse on the pilot and coal collection bin on the tender, SP No. 3803 stopped at El Paso, Texas in July 1940. Behind the AC-9 class engine is another survivor preserved at the California State Railroad Museum as of this writing. Southern Pacific No. 137, the company's Dynamometer Car used for performance testing and ratings, is coupled to No. 3803 to record the feedback of the test instruments. Malcom Gaddis photo, SPH&TS Collection

February and September 1937 as the AC-7 class. These featured a modern streamlined cab, Boxpok drivers, and larger rectangular tenders with a 22,030 gallon water capacity. The AC-8 class was delivered between August and November 1939, totaling 28 in number. The AC-8s were nearly identical to the AC-7, but were the first to feature air horns under the cab as an additional warning device. They were also 18,100 pounds heavier, had SP's patented spring pad lubricators, and featured a similar tender. The 220-R-3 tenders delivered with Class AC-8 were the first to feature the Pyle light mounted in the rear bulkhead, reducing the water capacity to 21,900 gallons.

The AC-8 class represented such a high measure of success for the railroad that SP ordered three nearly-identical classes from Baldwin during WWII. Forty AC-10 class locomotives in 1942, 30 AC-11s in 1942–1943, and 20 AC-12 class in 1943–1944. With these 90 AC types added to the roster, Southern Pacific's arsenal of cab-ahead articulated steam became the largest in the world. A total of 256 cab-in-front locomotives over a 34-year period represents the dominance of Southern Pacific in American Railroading and the development of the Western United States.

No study of Southern Pacific's Baldwin-built articulated engines would be complete without a mention of the dozen AC-9 class 2-8-8-4 conventional locomotives purchased from competitor Lima in 1939. Being the only shrouded (semi-streamlined) articulated steam locomotives ever built, No. 3800–3811 were some of the most powerful locomotives purchased by Southern Pacific. They were likewise bought to satisfy an uncommon fuel agreement on the Rio Grande Division, one that came with the acquisition of predecessor El Paso and Southwestern in 1924. That railroad had contracts with the Dawson coal fields in New Mexico to provide fuel to the railroad between El Paso, Texas and Tucumcari, New Mexico. With these provisions, the AC-9 class was delivered to burn coal. By 1950, the class was converted to oil and in the spring of 1953, all but No. 3800 was transferred to the Salt Lake Division at Sparks.

Southern Pacific did own other Mallet-type locomotives, which were in excess of the 256 cab-aheads. Additionally, a "Classification and Assignment" book issued March 1, 1943 revealed Southern Pacific reserved the 4700–4789 block of engine numbers in case there were future deliveries of cab-ahead type locomotives.

Like other steam fleets in America, the once-ubiquitous Malleys became fewer in number as their successors were delivered. Coming in the form of four-unit sets of diesel-electric locomotives manufactured by General Motors subsidiary Electro-Motive Division, or EMD, the F Units began replacing steam in great numbers by the mid-50s. 1953 was a year of great change for the assignment of the cab-aheads, with most of the 4100s being removed from the Salt Lake Division and assigned to more hospitable territory where good water was easier to find.

With every delivery of new diesel locomotives, more ACs were reassigned to the Coast and Western Divisions, with the last operating out of West Oakland and Tracy. On November 29–30, 1956, No. 4211 hauled the last revenue freight by a cab-ahead on the Western Division. A year later on November

Above: Southern Pacific F3A No. 6122, delivered in January 1948, leads an extra freight eastbound at Mojave shortly after being purchased. The track at right is the lead for the Owenyo Branch, referred to as the "Jawbone Line." Harvey Kelso photo, Southern Pacific Railroad History Center Collection

Above: On October 19, 1958 in conjunction with the last sanctioned standard gauge steam movement on the Southern Pacific, No. 4294 was officially dedicated for display in Sacramento. The Pacific Coast Chapter, Railway and Locomotive Historical Society, is to thank for the last steam locomotive purchased new by the railroad being saved. Scott Inman Collection

30 and December 1, 1957, the California-Nevada Railroad Historical Society operated the final run of a Malley using SP 4274 between Sacramento and Sparks. As the excursion passengers departed the train at Sacramento as the sun was setting, so did the fire extinguish on these machines for eternity.

Through the diligent efforts of the Pacific Coast Chapter, Railway and Locomotive Historical Society, Southern Pacific 4294 was saved and proudly displayed by the City of Sacramento. Formally Dedicated on October 19, 1958, this last Malley has been a source of pride for the city, the California State Railroad Museum, California State Parks, and Southern Pacific fans of all ages. Since 1981, the locomotive has been on permanent display inside the Museum of Railroad History at CSRM. In addition to displaying the 4294, CSRM also owns the first Southern Pacific steam and diesel locomotives as the *CP Huntington* and SP No. 1000 respectively. If the eventual retirement of the company's last diesel-electric locomotive, ex-SP AC4400CW No. 378, is acquired by CSRM, it will be the only railroad museum that could claim such a preservation achievement. No other railroad in the world has the same preservation potential as the Southern Pacific. After all, SP donated more steam locomotives for public display than any other American railroad.

This publication represents over a decade of technological research and living history contributions from men who operated and maintained these locomotives. CSRM Docents David Anderson and the late Russell O'Day began this work as a project to benefit museum docents. While this book is of mainly technical nature, this information is not readily available in other sources. Our goal is to provide the reader with a user's manual to the 4294, and help future generations better understand this important survivor. We hope you enjoy it!

Scott Inman is a life-long Southern Pacific historian, author, and California State Railroad Museum Docent. He serves as a Director of the Southern Pacific Historical and Technical Society; the Pacific Coast Chapter, Railway and Locomotive Historical Society; and the Southern Pacific Railroad History Center.

Facing Page, Bottom: On the last weekend of service for a Southern Pacific Malley, No. 4274 lead the California-Nevada Railroad Historical Society's "Sierra Daylight" excursion on November 30 and December 1, 1957. Seen paused for a photo run-by at the Lincoln Avenue Penryn Station, X4274 was eastbound with the excursion train in tow. Stan Kistler Photo

3: 4294 and the California State Railroad Museum

The California State Railroad Museum's (CSRM) Cab-forward No. 4294 is the last of a long line of truly remarkable locomotives. Unique to the Southern Pacific Railroad (SP), they were, in the words of Lucius Beebe, "... more than any other single property or characteristic, the identifying hallmark of this company." To say that the CSRM is fortunate to possess this last remaining SP Cab-forward locomotive would be, at the very least, an understatement.

This book is not intended to be a definitive study of all cab-forwards but rather a basic working information document specifically about No. 4294 to help those interested to better understand this powerful machine and its various components. Everyone interested in the cab-forward is urged to read Dr. Robert Church's *Cab Forward* where he stated that they were the product of Southern Pacific's superb engineering department, and George Harlan's *Those Amazing Cab Forwards* for more information on all of these locomotives.

The 4294 was retired in 1956 and it was donated to the City of Sacramento, California in October of 1958. For 11 years it was placed in front of the Southern Pacific Passenger (now Amtrak) Station in Sacramento where it suffered neglect, vandalism and general deterioration. Nominally the property of the City of Sacramento, it was assigned to the CSRM during the time that the museum was being planned. The CSRM did a "cosmetic" restoration in 1981, but due to many factors, not the least of which were boiler restoration, some missing parts, and unjustifiable costs, no plans were ever made to restore it to operational condition.

In early 1909 SP purchased two Mallet articulated steam locomotives from Baldwin Locomotive Works to be used for the ever-increasing freight and passenger traffic over the Sierra Nevada. A decision was made for them to be oil burners because oil was a low cost fuel, was readily available in California and because "it was thought coal would not burn fast enough to develop the full power of the locomotive" (Church, p. 14). Though the locomotives proved to have the power for the job, it was soon discovered that due to the approximately 40 miles of snow sheds and tunnels then in existence on the Donner Pass route, the smoke, gasses and heat spewed out by the up-front stacks threatened to asphyxiate the crews. (Crews working this route referred to it as "railroading in a barn.") Inspired by a North Pacific Coast Railroad turn of the century experimental locomotive, SP's engineering department designed a locomotive with the cab up front that would be safer for crews to operate in the Sierra Nevada environment. SP ordered fifteen of the new design from Baldwin taking delivery in February and March of 1910 without putting even one through a trial run.

These early articulated locomotives were of a compound steam design invented by Anitole Mallet, meaning that in addition to articulation they had both high and low pressure cylinders. High pressure was used in the cylinders of the front engine, and then the exhaust steam was used again in the low pressure cylinders of the rear engine. However, due to many problems, most compounds were converted to simple steam or scrapped by the late twenties. Thus the ACs (Articulated Consolidations) came into being. It should be noted that three of the compound Cab-forwards (4011, 4013, and 4022) were in use as late as 1936 when they were finally scrapped. Though the "AC" Cab-forwards were not true "Mallets" the name stuck and these locomotives were called "Malleys" by SP engineers and shop employees as long as they were operated.

It is also important to note that the decision to run these machines in the Cab-forward configuration produced a myriad of engineering problems brought on by the fact that they were not designed to pull heavy loads in reverse. Several features had to be re-engineered by Southern Pacific and Baldwin to insure this capability.

Diesel Locomotives were assigned on Overland Route passenger trains beginning in the mid-1930s. A decision was made by SP to purchase diesel locomotives in 1939. However, as WW II loomed, diesel engines were increasingly being manufactured for the military to power submarines, landing craft, and other military equipment. As a result very few diesel locomotives were allowed to be built between 1940 and 1945. The SP war-time work load was the greatest in the line's history and the need for tractive power was so great it had to continue to invest in steam. However, at the end of hostilities, SP began to purchase the much more economical diesel-electric locomotive. The company converted to diesel as rapidly as possible and, by doing so, spelled the doom of steam. This happened over a period of about 10 years from 1945 to 1956. AC 4294 was decommissioned in March of 1956 after only 12 years of service. The final revenue run of Cab-forwards in general was in November of that year. AC-12 No. 4294 was the last newly-purchased steam locomotive delivered to the Southern Pacific.

While Cab-forwards were not the largest US steam locomotives, they were the largest on SP's locomotive roster. Union Pacific's Big Boy was the largest steam locomotive in regular use (though not the largest ever built). The Big Boy was 132 feet long, a coal burner that produced 135,000 pounds of tractive force at the draw bar and was rated at 6,200 horsepower. In comparison, the 4294 is 125 feet long, an oil burner, produced a tractive force of 124,300 pounds and was rated at 6,000 horsepower. Interestingly, although only 25 Big Boys were built, eight of them have survived and are on display in various museums and parks around the country. In contrast 256 Cab-forwards were built and the 4294 is the sole survivor.

The early Mallet 16-drive-wheel Cab-forwards were designated MC for Mallet Consolidation. The later, simple-steam Cab-forwards were designated AC for Articulated Consolidation. SP had built 12 2-6-6-2 Cab-forwards designed for passenger service that were designated MM for Mallet Mogul. There were other designations for some early articulated locomotives, but they are not included in this work.

Reader's Note

Some redundancy is built into this document to reduce the reader's need to refer to prior statements. This technique is used to provide real-time clarity and to enhance the retention of the information. Also note that some of the measurements stated in the document may not be exact due to the difficulty in measuring them. There are still numerous items on the locomotive that have not been identified.

Figure 1 – Front End Details

A – Number board
B – Clear Vision window
C – Headlight
D – Air horn
E – Bell (concealed)
F – Air cooling screen
G – Coupler (type E-7)
H – Permanent snow plow pilot
I – "Extra" flag
J – Classification light
K – Saturated steam line to passenger cars
L – Flag or sign holder
M – Electrical outlet
N – Injector water line to check valve
O – Marker light holder
P – Injector

4: Locomotive Data

Drive Wheel Diameter	63 in.
Wheel Configuration	4-8-8-2
Cylinder Diameter	24 in.
Cylinder Stroke	32 in.
Overall Length (including tender)	124 ft. 9 in.
Height of the Locomotive above the rails	16 ft. 4 in.
Wheel Base of the Locomotive	67 ft. 3 in.
Wheel Base of the Drive Wheels	44 ft. 7 in.
Weight of the Locomotive	
boiler filled with water	657,900 Ib.
boiler empty	576,800 Ib.
on drivers	531,700 lb.
Boiler Water Capacity	10,935 gal.
Boiler Pressure	250 lb.
Fuel	Bunker C Oil (a viscous, heavy oil with a high BTU content)

Tender Weight

filled with water and oil	393,300 Ib.
empty	160,000 Ib.
Total Weight of Engine and Tender	1,051,000 Ib.

fully loaded with fuel oil and water (= 525.5 tons)

Tractive Effort	124,300 Ib. (at the draw bar)
Fire Box Temperature	1,700 Degrees (under heavy load)
Horsepower	6,000 (40 MPH; see Horsepower, p. 81)
Class Designation	AC 12 (Articulated Consolidation 12, the last (12th) group of articulated engines purchased)
Built	Finished March 1944 Built at the Baldwin Locomotive Works in Philadelphia, PA
Time to Construct	About two months The last locomotive of the final order for 20 AC 12's from Baldwin, thus they were built on an assembly line. All of the appliances were off the shelf items.)
Delivery to SP	March 1944
Service Time	12 Years

(4294 was decommissioned in March of 1956, to be replaced by more efficient diesel engines, especially EMD F7s. The normal service time of Cab-forward locomotives was 25 to 30 years.)

Initial Cost	$256,000

Note: All descriptions of features on this locomotive are based on the fact that the cab is the front, and the "right" and "left" sides are with respect to this arrangement. All temperatures are in Fahrenheit. "Wet steam" is an abbreviation for saturated steam, and "dry steam" is an abbreviation for superheated steam.

Engineering Problems

When SP and Baldwin designed the Cab-forwards in 1909 they had to work out the numerous engineering changes. This is not a complete list; it only covers the major problems.

1. The front truck had to be altered. The draw bars and the chafing plate had to be removed and replaced with a conventional coupling, pilot beam and the pilot.
2. The fireman's and engineer's seats had to be relocated along with all of the controls, gauges and all other necessary features. This was an important part of the new design. It was necessary in order to relocate the engineer to the right side of the cab.
3. The front of the cab had to be closed in, and running lights, lighted number boards, emergency running light holders, electrical receptacles, an air horn and a bell had to be installed.
4. Because the firebox was now separated by a great distance from the tender, the following pipelines had to be added along the sides of the locomotive:
   - Train line (pipe) along the right side.
   - Cold water line from the tender to the injector on the left side.
   - Oil line from the tender to the fire box.
   - Saturated steam line on the left side from the turret to the tender, for the passenger car heat.
   - Saturated steam line from the turret to the tender oil heater.
   - Compressed air line from the cab to the tender for a water level gauge.
   - Cold water line from the cold water pump to the feed water heater.
5. The brake shoes, and the gear that held them, had to be moved to the rear of the drivers, and the sand pipes had to be moved to conform to the new location of the brake shoes.
6. The rear truck had to be strengthened and fitted with a draw bar unit and a chafing plate.
7. The monkey deck had to be designed, constructed and installed along with its railing.
8. The throttle linkage had to be relocated to the right side and a rocker installed to allow it to operate in a conventional manner.
9. Miscellaneous piping under the cab floor had to be rerouted from the right side of the cab to the left side, and vice versa. This was part of the task of switching the engineer and fireman to the opposite sides.

Use of Steam and Air

The use of steam generated from the locomotive's boiler, and compressed air from the air pumps on the rear of the locomotive, not only provided for the propulsion of the train, but they also helped make life easier and more efficient for the engineer and fireman. The following list breaks down, and gives details of, how each source of energy is used and controlled. It includes the page location of the control facilities within the locomotive (in *red* italics), as well as the location of related descriptions within the document.

SUPER-HEATED STEAM (DRY STEAM)

Control locations:

Feed pump system: Fireman's side (reach rod) – Feed water transfer pump (p.25, 62, 73, 76) – Feed pump (p.25, 34, 62, 63)

Blower: Fireman's side *Dry steam header* (p.36, 41, 53)

Fuel oil atomizer: In the oil nozzle in the fire box (p.36, 41, 53)

Tender fuel-oil blow-back: Fireman's side *Overhead appliance rack* (p.36)

Air compressors: Reach rod, left side of locomotive (p.35, 41, 58)

Steam whistle: Engineer's side (p.26, 29, 41, 42)

SATURATED STEAM (WET STEAM)

Injector steam supply: *Overhead appliance rack* (p.44)

Cab heaters: Fireman's side (p.31, 33, 38, 41)

Cylinder cocks: Engineer's side (p.31, 41)

Fuel oil heater (coil type) in tender: Fireman's side *Overhead appliance rack* (p.36, 44)

Injector water supply and freeze prevention: Fireman's side *Overhead appliance rack* (p.41, 45)

Passenger car steam heat: *Overhead appliance rack* (p.41, 43, 44, 45)

Power reversing system: *Overhead appliance rack* (p.39, 43, 50, 68)

Hydrostatic lubricator: *Overhead appliance rack* (p.43, 44)

Note: this system exists but was *not* connected; lubrication was done by other means. There was no hydrostatic lubrication.

Fireman's wet steam manifold supply line: *Overhead appliance rack* (p.43)

Fuel oil heater (engineer's side): Inline fuel oil heater, right side of locomotive (below cab) (p.36, 41)

Fuel oil heater (fireman's side): Inline fuel oil heater, left side of locomotive (above 5th and 6th drivers) (p.36)

Cab steam heat: *Overhead appliance rack* (p.31, 33, 38)

Left-side boiler water level sight glass: *Overhead appliance rack* (p.30, 31)

Injector steam supply line: *Overhead appliance rack* (p.43, 44)

Dynamo (electric generator and turbine) steam: *Overhead appliance rack* (p.37, 41, 44, 45)

AIR CONTROLS

Air horn: Engineer's side (p.19, 29, 40)

Steam whistle control: Engineer's side (p.22, 23, 26, 29, 40, 41, 42, 56)

Window defrosters: *Circular air manifold* (p.30, 31, 33)

Sand controls: Engineer's side (p.40, 41)

Bell: Fireman's side *Circular air manifold* (p.23, 30)

Respirators: Fireman's side *Circular air manifold* (p.30)

8.ET Westinghouse air system and brake stand: Engineer's side (p.29, 58, 59, 60)

Emergency brake: Fireman's side (p. 34)

Driver wheel and tender wheel water sprayers: Engineer's side (missing) (p.33, 67)

Signal pot (conductor-engineer communication): Engineer's side (p.22, 41)

Tender oil tank air pressure supply: Fireman's side (p.36, 64)

Tender water tank level indicator gauge: Fireman's side *Circular air manifold* (p.35)

5: Exterior Features

Air Brake and Communication Systems: On the front of the locomotive and the back of the tender there are two hoses (see Figure 2 below). The larger one is the train line (pipe) used for the air brake system that runs the length of the train. The smaller one is the signal hose, and was used for communication to the engineer from the passenger train conductors, snow plow foremen, etc. There were no signal lines on freight trains.

The passenger train conductor communicated with the engineer using a whistle code to notify him that the train was to get under way (or to stop), the car heat needed to be increased or decreased, the speed was to be increased or reduced, or to make an unscheduled stop, etc. The system worked only one way: from the conductor to the engineer using the signal air-line (see "Signal Pot," p.41). The engineer communicated back with the conductor using the whistle, throttle, and (on passenger trains only) using the appliance controls.

Air Reservoirs: There are two located under the cab floor. The larger one is the wet reservoir and the smaller one is the dry reservoir (see "Air Reservoirs," p.58, 59).

Glad Hands: The glad hands are the metal connectors on the train line connection hoses. They are fitted with rubber connector bushings. Although the train brake and signal hoses are of a different size, they could in an emergency be connected to bypass a leaky train line pipe on an individual car (see Figure 2 below).

Air Filters: There are two 'Type G' air filters, one on either side of the engine above the fourth drivers (see Figure 39, p.68). Each canister is fitted with a cleanable filter and connected to the air pumps (compressors) through 3 inch pipes. They are located forward of the exhaust stacks to prevent smoke and exhaust gasses from fouling the air being compressed.

Air Horn: The Tyfon air horn is located on the front of the

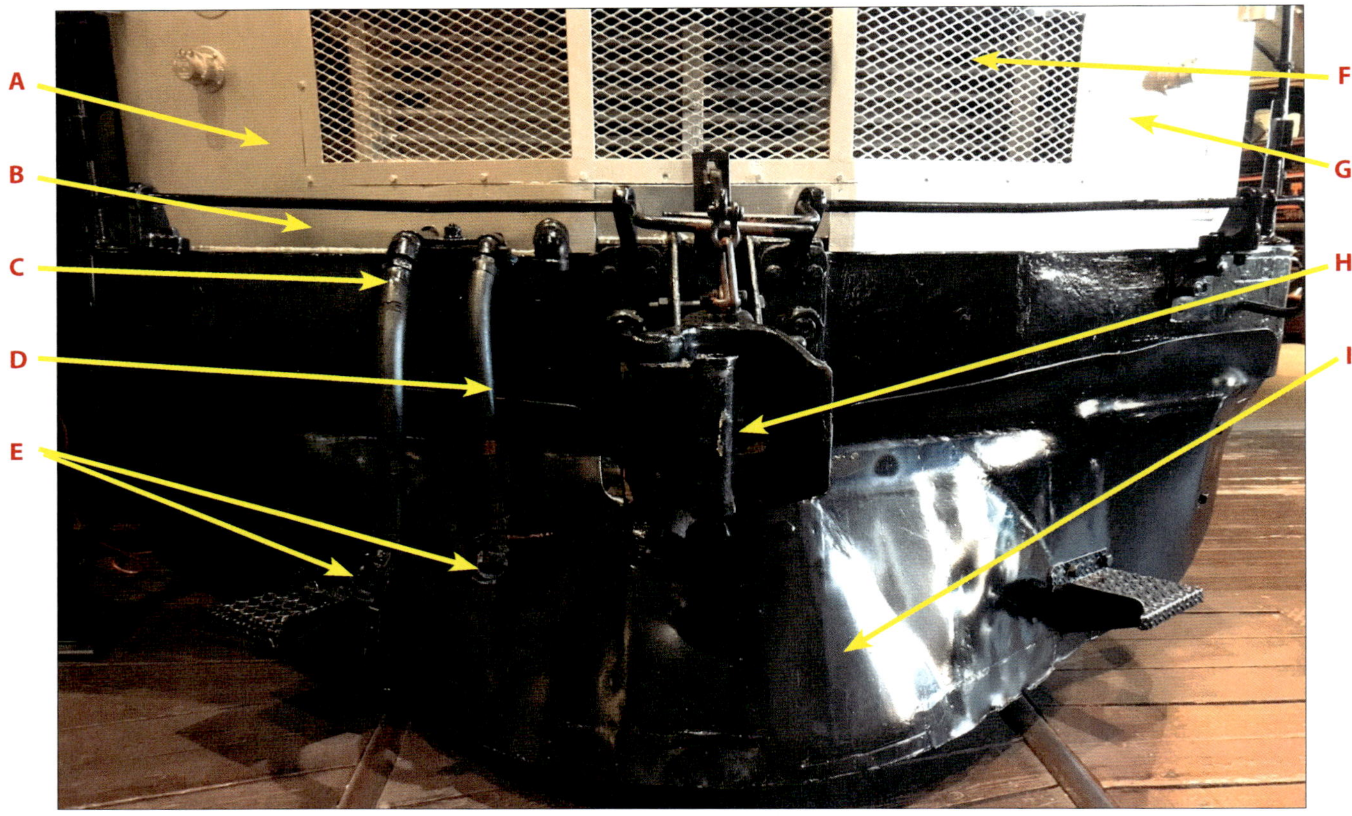

Figure 2 – Pilot Detail

Scott Inman photo

A – Cut bar lever (uncoupler)
B – Pilot beam
C – Train line brake hose (larger)
D – Signal hose (smaller)
E – Glad hands
F – Air cooling screen
G – Aluminum paint
H – Coupler
I – Pilot

locomotive. The horn was air activated by a valve (missing on the 4294) located just behind the steam whistle control valve just beside the engineers seat. Air horns were installed on Cab-forwards starting with AC-8s. The air horn was used at grade crossings because it was more effective (see "Whistle," p.26; see also Figure 28, p.56).

Bell: The bell, located behind and above the grill on the right front of locomotive, was air operated from the right side of the fireman's seat, activated by a Transportation Devices Corporation bell ringer. People who have heard these bells claim that they sounded "dull." The dull sound can possibly be attributed to the fact that the locomotive was built during World War II and thus the shortage of copper and brass during that time.

Boards (Number Boards): Located on each side of the upper front of the cab, they were equipped with back lights and displayed train numbers. When running "extra" (not scheduled) an "X" was placed in front of each number. Southern Pacific manufactured its own number plates. The letters were rounded, not sharp or flat and allegedly easier to read.

Boiler Blow-Down Spreaders: The two rectangular spreaders are located just behind and to the outside of the front trucks about a foot above the ties (see Figure 3, p.24). This apparatus is described in detail in the chapter on boilers (see "Blow-off/ Blow-down Apparatus," p.52).

Brake Pipe Vent Valve: This device is located above the gap between the third and fourth drivers on the right side of the locomotive. It was used to insure quick action during an emergency train separation (see "Brake Pipe Vent Valve," p.60).

Cab Configuration

Note: Only sloping cab and cab construction material are under the sub-heading of "cab configuration."

Sloping Cab: The forward slope on the lower back of the cab was introduced in 1910. This configuration, Also known as a sport cab, allowed the changing of boiler stay bolts without the removal of the cab.

Cab Construction Material: The cab is made of steel plate and lined on the inside with wood for insulation. The original floor consisted of wooden planks, which are now covered with plywood.

Cooling Screen: Starting with AC-8s in 1939 an opening on the lower front of the cab was fitted with a screen to allow air to flow over the compressed air cooling coil, which is installed directly behind the screen. The cooling screens were enlarged starting in 1942 on AC-10s (see Figure 2, p.22).

Cooling Coil: The compressed air cooling coil is behind the screen on the front of the cab. Its functional place in the system is between the wet and dry reservoirs. When air is being compressed it heats, up absorbing water vapor contained within the air. Thus the need for a cooler to aid in the removal of the water before it enters the dry reservoir. There is an inline water removal pot located between the air cooler and the dry reservoir. (see Figure 2, p.22; see also "Inter Air Cooler,"p.58).

Rounded Cab: Starting with AC-7s in 1938, the front of the cabs were constructed in a three-panel semicircle. This created a sleeker look, allowed more room for the front end brakeman's jump seat and allowed the bell to be placed under the cab floor. It also allowed the train numbers to be changed from inside the cab. Prior to AC-7s, the front of the cabs were flat with the bell mounted outside.

Aluminum Paint on Cab Front: Starting in June of 1946, SP painted an aluminum colored strip about 3 feet tall across the lower front of the cab just above the pilot beam. This increased visibility at a distance and was part of a safety program that would make locomotives more visible.

Couplers: There are two automatic Type E7 self-closing couplers: one on the front of the cab and one on the end of the tender. When 4294 was operational they were left un-painted to make it easier to see cracks. Each coupler is operated with a cut lever on either side (see Figure 2, p.22).

Density Light: A light was installed just to the right of the smoke stacks allowing the fireman to check the density of the smoke at night (see Figure 30, p.58). To do so, he would have to lean out of the cab window. It has been said that the light was not very effective because it was usually covered with soot. This light is always illuminated for visitors, and can be seen toward the rear of the locomotive.

Dry Steam Header: There is a dry steam header on the left side of the smoke box. It is tapped directly into the super heater header and extends down the side of the smoke box to just below the left side catwalk. It supplied dry steam to the air compressors, the cold water pump, feed water pump, and to a dry steam header in the cab via an insulated line that extends forward under the boiler insulation (see Figure 28, p.56).

Electric Generator (Dynamo): The Pyle National Turbo 800 watt type Dynamo (32V.D.C.) is located just behind and to the right of the turret. It consists of a small saturated steam turbine powering an electric generator. It supplied all of the electricity needed by the locomotive. Many photographs of steam locomotives show a steam feather from the exhaust of the electric dynamo turbine.

Electric Outlets: There are two female electrical outlets on either side of the front of the cab. They are marked and rated at: 30 amps D.C., 250V.A.C. and 125V.D.C. They were used to supply electrical power to the stand-by rear marker lights

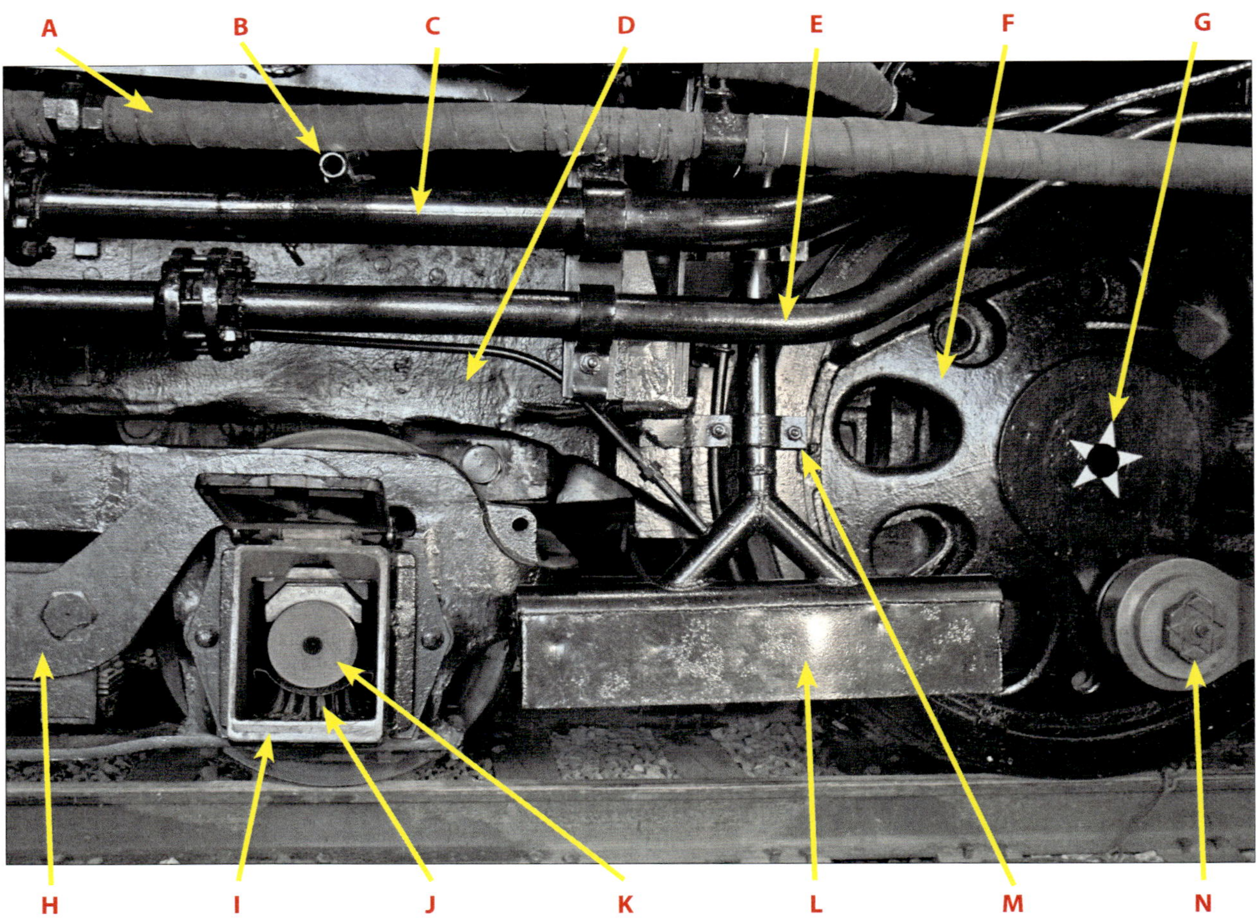

Figure 3 – Front Under-cab Detail
(Fireman's Side)

A – Oil line from tender
B – Steam supply point
C – Injector water feed line
D – Engine casting
E – Injector discharge line to check valve
F – Boxpok drive wheel
G – Star indicates internal bearing and denotes type of axle lubrication
H – Front truck frame
I – Journal box & oil reservoir
J – Springs with wicks to distribute oil to the axle
K – Truck axle
L – Blow-down spreader (defuser)
M – Tire retaining safety clip
N – Side rod pin.

when they were in use. The marker lights would be used if the locomotive was to be run backwards over a considerable distance. Otherwise they were stored in a tool box on the tender. Note the marker light holders on each side of the cab front (see "Running Lights," p.26; see also Figure 16, p.39).

Exhaust Splitter: The cast iron exhaust splitter is located just above the exhaust stacks (see Figure 28, p.56). It diverted the upward force of the exhaust, directing it away at about a 45° angle to the gaps in the upper corners of the flat roof snow sheds. It helped prevent the exhaust gasses from fouling the air in the snow sheds and the full force of the exhaust from damaging the overhead wooden beams and sheeting in the sheds.

Fireman's Seat: Retired firemen state that they usually sat in their seat with their back to the side window so they could focus on the gauges. They also spent a lot of time leaning out of the window to look at the smoke. A right side arm rest on the fireman's seat was not installed on operating AC locomotives in order to allow a sideways seating position.

Flag Holders: There are two flag holders on the front of the cab. They are above and near the running lights.

Flags: White flags and white running lights indicated that the engine was pulling an unscheduled extra train. (An unscheduled extra train also had an "X" before the train

A – Feed water system control handle
B – Note the notch in the handle rim for the fireman to track his last adjustment
C – Dry and saturated steam header valve handle console
D – Firing lever

Figure 4 – Fireman's Seat & Controls

number on the number boards.) Green flags and green running lights (marker lights) were used to announce that another section of a regular scheduled train would follow. Red flags to be used in emergencies, or for flagging ahead or behind the train, were also kept in the cab.

Flag Holders (Blue): There are two pipes, 14 inches long and 1 inch in diameter, mounted on either side of the cab between the flag holders and the pilot beam. They could have been used to hold blue "MEN AT WORK" sheet metal signs to be displayed when the locomotive was immobilized and being worked on. The signs were fixed with a metal rod which could also be pushed into the ballast or affixed to the track.

Headlights: There are two Pyle-National headlights: one on the front of the cab and one on rear of tender.

Inspection Ports: There is an inspection port on either side of the front of the cab, about 6 inches in diameter with hinged metal covers. Their use is unknown.

Monkey Deck: The monkey deck is the platform between the engine and the tender. On some early models, while rounding curves in tunnels and snow sheds, the rear corners of monkey decks would contact the walls. Thus extended corners had to be tapered to allow clear passage. Note that the monkey deck on the 4294 is not tapered (see photos, p.61). This deck was not a safe place to ride as scalding water occasionally showered the deck and the smoke and exhaust gasses in tunnels could be insufferable. Note the railings on each side are made up of three sections placed in an open "U" configuration. The probable reason for the "U" shape is to add stability to the railing.

Pilot (Snow Plow): The McCormack pilot (the sheet metal unit below the front coupler) used on earlier ACs was replaced with a ¼ in. thick sheet of pressed steel starting with the AC-8s in 1939 (see Figure 2, p.22). This device is essentially a snowplow and was used to move light, fresh snow off the track. Sometimes the solid metal pilots were called "deflecting pilots" or "pilot plows." A Cab-forward could run through about one foot of fresh powder snow.

Running Lights (Classification Lights, Marker Lights): There is a set of Pyle-National running lights on the front of the cab. They can be switched from white to green with a small lever on the side of each light. The back of the tender is equipped with marker lights that can be rotated to show red or green to the rear. They have a red lens on one side and green lenses on the other three sides. Red was shown to the rear while the locomotive was on a main track. They were turned to green if the train was on a side track.

Welded on top of the pilot beam on each side of the front of the cab are two marker light holders. If the locomotive for some reason was running backwards marker lights could be brought forward from a tool box on the tender and installed on the holders, and they could be rotated to show red to the rear. Electrical power to these lights would come from the nearby female electrical outlets (see "Electrical Outlets," p.23). Note that these holders also have a place for red flags.

Sand Boxes: There is a sand box (sand dome) on top of the boiler over each set of drive wheels. Each has two filler hatches and a capacity of one ton of sand. Sand was delivered to the track at a point just in front of the first three drivers of each engine through three pipes that extend downward on each side of the boiler. The pipes are partially covered below by the boiler insulation. Earlier ACs had sand pipes for each driver. Air activated sand traps on each sand pipe just below the sand domes allowed sand to flow down the pipes and onto the rails (see Interior Cab Features chapter, p. 29; see also Figure 17, p.40).

Smoke Stacks: There are two – one for the front engine and one for the rear engine. Exhaust temperature from the stacks was about 450 degrees F.

Steam

Steam Dome: It is on the center top of boiler, and is smaller than the two sand domes. It is the highest part of the boiler and the source of steam for the super heater, and ultimately for propulsion. The steam dome could possibly have contained a tangential steam dryer, but most tangential steam dryers were removed during the 1950s.

Saturated (Wet) Steam: Saturated steam was delivered to a turret header from a nipple welded into the boiler below the turret cowling on the top center of the locomotive (see Figure 21, p.45).

Super-Heated (Dry) Steam Line: Super-heated steam was delivered via a 2-inch insulated line that was tapped into the upper part of the smoke box on the left side of the locomotive (see Figure 28, p.56). It extends downward supplying steam to several appliances. One offshoot extends forward just above the walk on the left side of the locomotive, then forward under the boiler insulation into the cab. It supplied dry steam directly to the fireman's dry steam header.

Feed Pump Water Heater Hatch: There is a large rectangular hatch bolted on the top of the smoke box that provides access to the feed pump water heater.

Turret (Boiler Head): The turret consists of a cowling located just behind the cab on top of the boiler. The cowling covers a wet steam manifold which disbursed wet steam as required for numerous engine appliances (see Figure 21, p.45).

Whistle: The whistle is located just forward of, and a little left of, the exhaust smoke stacks on the super heater header (see Figure 28, p.56).On early models it was air controlled, thus its tone could not be altered like a hand operated whistle. It was either on or off. However, SP engineers eventually developed a six-tone (aka chime) melodious air-operated whistle that could be played like a hand-operated whistle. The actual control valve (made of brass) is just to the left of the engineer's seat (see Figure 6, p.29).

A – Cab roof ventilator handle

B – Fireman's boiler water level sight glass

C – Wet steam line from turret to fireman's wet steam header

D – Boiler cleanout plugs

Figure 5 – Fireman's Seat & Controls

Above: Controls on right side of fireman's seat.

6: Interior Cab Features

Engineer's Side

Air Brake Controls

Air Pressure Gauges: The Quadraplex air gauge is located on the left side and for- ward of the engineer's seat. It is the rectangular box containing two dials with two pressure indicators on each dial (see "Air Pressure Gauges," p.59; see also the Brake System chapter, p.58).

Brake Pedestal (Stand): The train brake pedestal is a Westinghouse Model 8-ET brake valve. It is located just to the left front of the engineer's seat. For details see "Brake Pedestal," p.59.

Engine Brake Control Handle (Independent Brake): The smaller independent, or "engine," brake is the top handle on the train brake stand. It was used to brake the locomotive

Figure 6 – Air Brake Control Stand

when it was not connected to a train or was moving only a few cars. It operated both the locomotive and tender brakes.

Train Brake Control Handle (Automatic Brake): The automatic, or "train", brake handle is located lower on the air brake stand. It was used to control the brakes on the entire train. It is the larger of the two brake handles.

Air Horn Control Valve: This valve was located left of the engineer's seat just behind the steam whistle control valve. Note the hold to the left of the whistle control where this valve was located.

Air Manifold (round): There is a vertical circular manifold on the fireman's right side with four exposed threaded nipples. Each nipple was affixed with a brass valve, and they were used for the following: (1) the bell, (2) the four air respirator attachment heads, (3) the front window hot air defrosters and (4) tender water tank level indicator. (Note: these are labels molded into the manifold.) All of these appliances were connected to the four missing valves with copper tubes, which are also missing.

Air Respirator Equipment: All of the respiratory equipment is missing. There are respirator supply points for at least four persons. The breathing apparatus consisted of a sponge in a cone shaped funnel affixed on the end of an air hose. Air was supplied from the main dry air reservoir. The air passed through a pressure reducing valve and a filter before it was made available to the crew. The respirators gave crew members in the cab of mid-train and rear-end helper engines access to clean air in the snow sheds and tunnels.

Respirator Manifolds: The small pipe manifold with two shiny brass caps, just to the right front of the fireman's seat, supplied air to both the fireman's and front-end brakeman's air respirators. The engineer's and a fourth respirator connection is just behind the engineer's seat. They were all connected to the fireman's circular air manifold by copper tubing which is missing.

Engineer's Gauges: Most of the engineer's gauges are identified in Figure 7, p.31. They include, from right to left, the Quadraplex Air Gauge, the Exhaust and Steam Back Pressure Gauge and the Speedometer. The Ashcroft Pilot Gauge, and the Boiler Foam Alarm device, further to the left, are missing. One of the missing gauges is the Steam Temperature Gauge that shows the steam temperature as it leaves the super heater.

Valve Pilot Gauge (Cut Off Gauge): The original gauge, made by Ashcroft, is missing on the 4294. It was located on the engineer's side just ahead of the boiler foam alarm device. It indicated the cut-off percentage (length of the stroke of the valve pistons) which gave the engineer a visual guide to best determine how to regulate the valve motion and control the cut-off (the amount of steam admitted to the main cylinders). Steam was only admitted for part of the stroke. After the cut-off point, the expanding steam pushed the piston to the full stroke.

When starting on grades with heavy trains, a delayed cut-off would admit more steam and give more power as needed. The piping of this gauge could be switched so that the cylinders of one engine could be cut out and readings made on the second. Prior to its development engineers would adjust the valve piston stroke by the sound of the engine and a lot of savvy based on experience.

It is possible that an Ashcroft 1043 gauge was installed instead of the one described above. This gauge was a much simpler device, consisting of a pair of Bourdon gauges whose needles formed an acute angle that gave the engineer a visual guide to best determine how to regulate the stroke of the valve pistons.

Automatic Train Control Magnet: This device was a safety feature designed to stop the locomotive and the train before it could get into trouble in the event that the crew missed a red signal in a severe snow storm or were incapacitated. Located below the cab, it could sense a set of magnets located between the rails. If the engineer failed to activate an override forestalling the mechanism prior to crossing the magnets, the train would automatically come to a stop. To reset the device someone would have to throw a lever below the cab floor. The override control handle was made of brass and was located on a 4 inch by 1 foot rectangular box just in front of the engineer's main gauges. The brackets that held the magnet are still in place below the cab.

Boiler Foam Alarm: (Signal Foam Meter) This device was located on the right side of the cab, just to the left of the engineer's seat, but it has been removed. It detected foam above the water level in the boiler. It was a rectangular box with a yellow light in the top half and a red light in the bottom half. It was connected to two electrodes placed in the upper part of the boiler. If foaming occurred a current would flow between the electrodes and the yellow light would glow. When foaming became critical the red light would glow. This meter is missing on the 4294. It may have been removed before the locomotive was taken out of service.

Boiler Water Level Sight Glass: There are two Sargent lighted water sight glasses, one on each side of the cab where they could be easily seen by both the engineer and the fireman (see Figure 8, p.32, engineer's side; see also Figure 12, p.35, fireman's side). They displayed the level of the water above the fire box crown sheet. Both glasses are connected to the boiler through two nipples welded directly into the boiler back head and two nipples welded to the top of the boiler. They are lighted with a tube light that fits into a receptacle behind the glass. Note the maximum and minimum water levels marked on the side panels, which were not to be surpassed while

A – Boiler steam pressure gauge

B – Barco speedometer (with speed recorder box above)

C – Throttle lever

D – Brake stand console

E – Duplex (exhaust and steam pipe) back pressure gauge

F – Power reversing lever pressure control) ("Johnson bar")

G – Quadraplex air pressure gauges

H – Drinking water cooler bracket

Figure 7 – Engineer's Gauges

climbing or descending a grade. There is also a drain on each water glass, allowing the glass to be cleaned through a drain below the cab floor. While running on level track the fireman would maintain the water level at about one half of the water glass depending on the situation. Each water glass unit has a built-in safety drain to drain away water and steam if the glass breaks. There is a possibility that these are not the original water sight glasses. Reflex glasses were always used on the ACs.

Boiler Test Cocks (Boiler Water Level Manual Test Indicator): There are three valves (tri-cocks) behind, above and to the right of the engineer's seat (see Figure 8, p.32). They could be used, if needed, to provide a manual check on the boiler water level. A manual check was useful to check the sight glasses if there was a question about the water level in the boiler. If opening valve produced water, the water level in the boiler was above the intake nipple to the boiler. If steam was produced, the intake nipple was above the water- steam interface. The bottom cock is located 3 inches above the boiler crown sheet.

Cab Windows: The front windows are 3/8", and the side windows are 5/16"-thick safety glass. There are also two narrow hinged (Clear Vision) storm windows above the engineers and fireman's windows. They were also used as vents (see "Clear Vision Windows" at right).

Cab Heaters: There are two. They are located just under the front windows on the inside of the cab (see Figure 9 and Figure 10, p.33). Steam is delivered through a 1¼ inch pipe from the turret manifold into a coil of 1¼ inch pipe. The control valves are separate, with one behind the engineer's seat and one behind the fireman's seat. Condensate from both coils is drained away in a 1¼ inch pipe to the spreader on the left side of the engine. Both heaters are fixed with a safety screen to prevent burns.

Cab Window Defrosters: There are two (one on top of each heater), each consisting of a ½ inch pipe with a series of 1/16 inch holes at about one inch spacing drilled along the top of the pipe (see Figure 9 and Figure 10, p.23). These defroster pipes are welded atop of the 1¼ inch cab heater coil. Compressed air was supplied through a ¼ inch copper tube attached alongside the cab heater coil. This air, heated by the cab heater pipes, was directed upwards onto the windows through the small holes in the ½ inch pipe to defrost the window. The control valve was located to the right of the fireman's seat, on the round air manifold (see "Air Manifold," p.30).

Clear Vision Windows: There is a unique feature that is part of the windows directly in front of the engineer's and the fireman's seats. Because there are no windshield wipers, there had to be a method for them to see the tracks ahead when it was raining or snowing. Both windows have a separate top panel that can be tilted outward leaving an open area where the engineer and the

A – Engineer's sight glass

B – Boiler test cocks ("tri-cocks")

C – Boiler back head

D – Sight glass drain valve

E – Cylinder cock valve

F – Boiler test cocks drain valves

Figure 8 – Engineer's Boiler Back Head Controls

fireman could have an unobstructed view in inclement weather. When in use, some water or snow would find its way into the cab but not enough to cause any problems. They were mostly used as vents.

Cylinder Cock Handle: There is a valve mostly behind and above the engineer's seat marked "Cylinder Cock" (see Figure 8, p.32). The cylinder cocks (one on each end of each cylinder) were opened with this valve before the locomotive was put into motion. They caused the removal of any water (condensate) that had accumulated in the cylinders while the locomotive was sitting idle. This was necessary to prevent damage to the cylinder heads, pistons and piston rods.

A – Injection water supply valve

B – Tool holders

C – Windshield defroster

D – Cab heater

E – Illuminated locomotive number board light housing

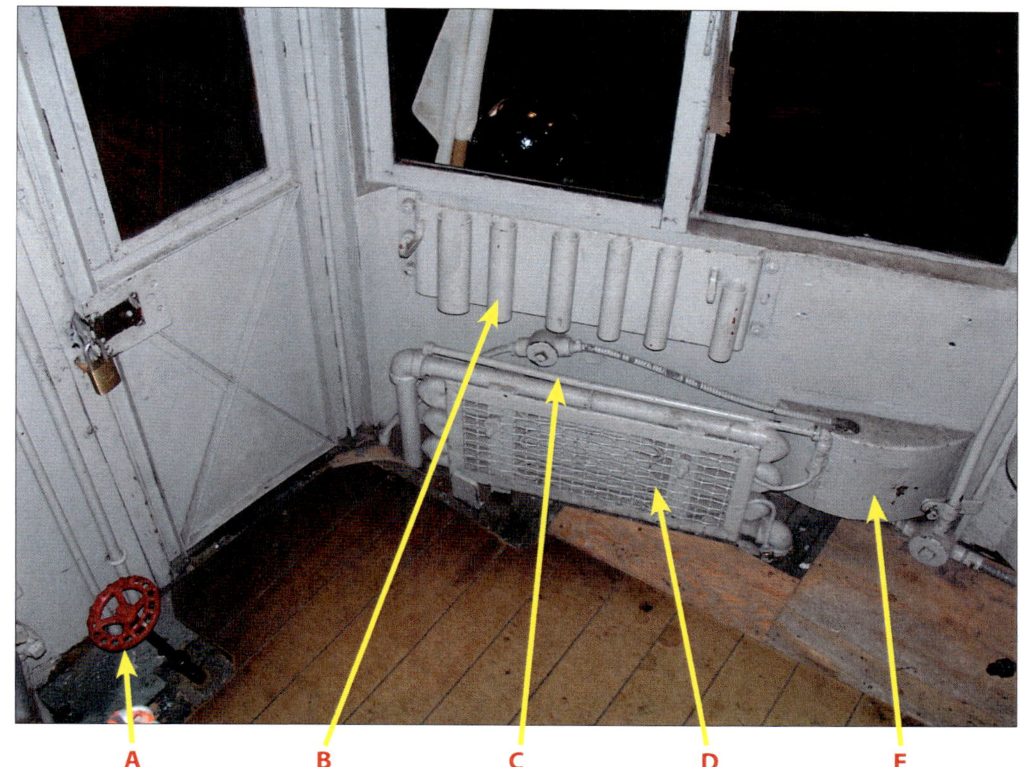

Figure 9 – Cab Interior, Fireman's Side

A – Drinking water cooler bracket

B – Torpedo & fusee container

C – Utility shelf

D – Headlight housing

E – Cab heater

Figure 10 – Cab Interior, Engineer's Side

Drinking Water Container: The container was a wood-insulated, rectangular metal can which was divided into two parts. One was filled with water, and the other ice if needed. The shelf that held it in place is still there on the inside center of the front cab wall (see Figure 10 above).

Driver Tire Cooling Water Spray Valve: Water was sprayed on all of the drivers to cool them during heavy braking. This was necessary especially when the locomotive was running downhill because the cast iron brake shoes could elevate the temperature of the steel tires causing them to expand and possibly loosen. The location of the air-activated valve needed to operate this system was on the engineer's side to the rear of the sanding valves. It has been removed from the locomotive. The tender wheels also have cooling water sprayers that are part of this system (see "Tender Cooling Water Sprayers," p.67).

Exhaust and Steam Back Pressure Gauge: This gauge is located on the right side of the cab just to the left of the engineer's seat (see Figure 7, p.31). This gauge allowed the engineer to track and adjust the back pressure if needed. If the back pressure was too high, it was using too much steam.

Fireman's Side

Emergency Brake Control: It is painted red and located on the left side of the cab above and directly to the rear of the left side door (see Figure 11 below). This device could be used by the fireman or the front-end brakeman to stop the train in an emergency.

Feed Water Pump Control: This control is the large notched valve handle located on the right of and above the fireman's seat (see Figure 4, p.25). The notch allowed the fireman to easily track the last adjustment. It controlled the amount of water injected into the boiler by the Worthington feed water pump system. It also supplied steam to the cold water pump between the locomotive and the tender. The feed water pump is located on the end of the smoke box just below the two air compressors (see "Feed Water Pump," p.62).

Feed Water Heater Gauge (Water Injection Rate): This gauge is located on the back wall of the boiler just above the fire box door next to the tender tank water level indicator (see Figure 12 at right). It is calibrated from 0 to 50 in gallons per minute. It showed the fireman that the pump was working and that water was entering the boiler.

Tender Water Tank Level Indicator: This gauge is also located on the back wall of the boiler just above the fire box door, to the left of the Feed Water Heater Gauge (see Figure 12 at right). By forcing air into the bottom of the tender water tank, a number representing the weight of the remaining water, could be obtained which could be used to indicate the amount of water in the tank. It has been said this system did not work very well.

Figure 11 – Fireman's Emergency Brake Control

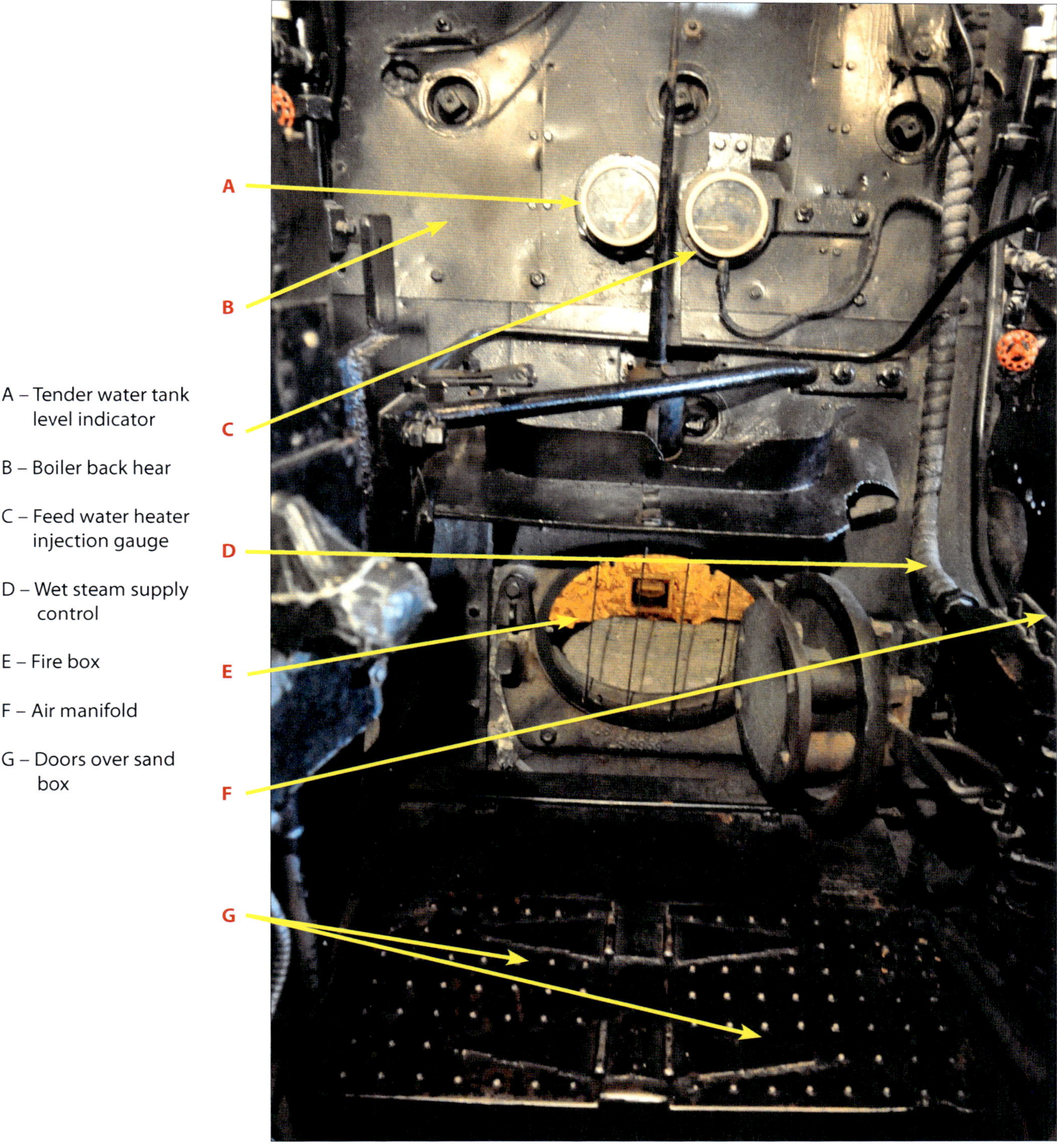

Figure 12 – Fireman's Gauges on Boiler Back Head

Fire Box Air Damper Control: On the right side of the firemen's seat is a 1½ inch, open ended, vertical pipe with two slots cut into its lip (see Figure 14, p.37). The pipe is fitted with a chain and a grab ring. The pipe extends below the cab floor and curves to the rear ending about 1½ feet from a rectangular damper (a metal flap about 8 inches by 2½ feet) on the lower front of the fire box. The chain extends from the pipe to the damper. The fireman could adjust (open or close) the damper by pulling or releasing of the chain, then securing it by slipping a link into a slot. This controlled the amount of air entering the fire box (see the "Boiler, Fire Box, Smoke Box, Super Heater & Steam Lines" chapter, p.52).

Fireman's Console Steam Control Valves: There are three valve handles on the upper dry steam header, and four valve handles on the lower wet steam header Both headers are located on the right side of the fireman's seat.

Super-Heated (Dry) Steam Header (Top 3 Valves)

Blower (Large Handle): The first valve (large diameter handle) on the top row is the blower control valve. It

Fuel Oil Atomizer (Oil Burner Nozzle): The second valve controlled the dry steam jet that atomized the fuel oil just before it entered the fire box. The steam expanded the surface of the oil allowing it to completely flash into flame as it entered into the fire box.

Fuel Oil Blow-back: The last (third) valve was used to clear the oil line from the cab to the tender This was necessary after the locomotive had been shut down for some time as the low specific gravity Bunker C oil would congeal. (see Figure 13 C below).

A – Valve for oil tank pressure

Upper Header (dry steam) valves:

B – Fuel oil atomizer

C – Fuel oil blow-back to the tender

D – Blower (large handle

Lower header (wet steam) valves:

E – Fuel oil heater; left side of loco (handle is not visible)

F – Fuel oil heater, right side of loco

G – Tender fuel oil heater valve

H – Tender water line freeze prevention

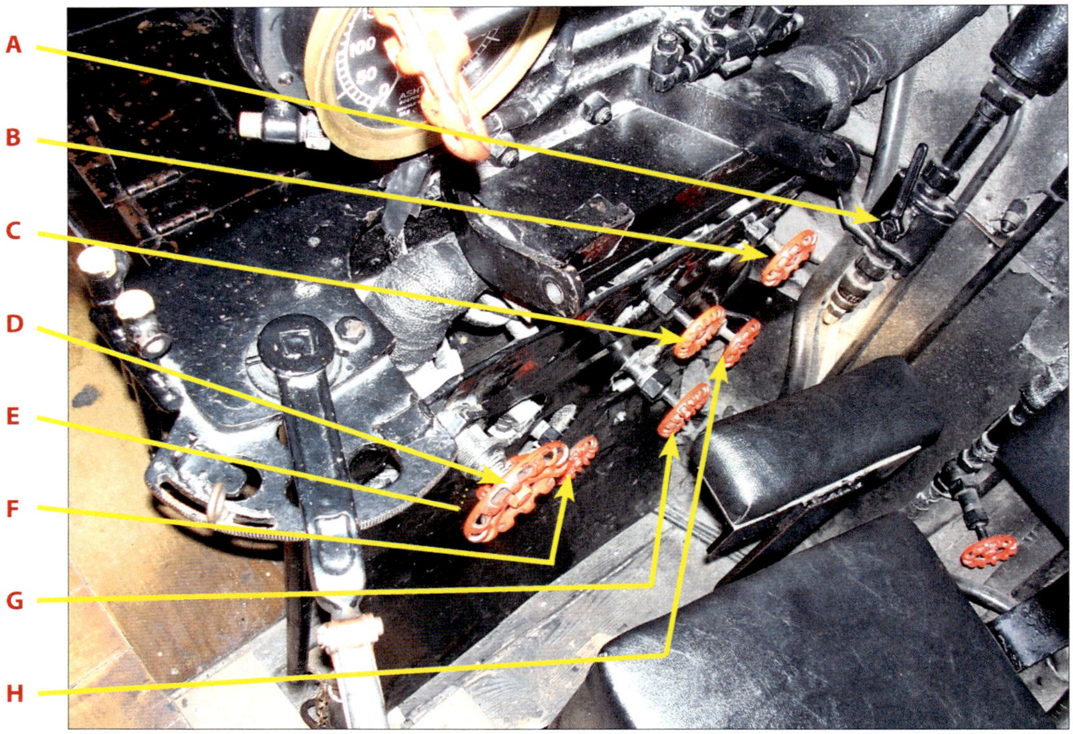

Figure 13 – Fireman's Console Steam Control Valves

controlled the steam ring jets that are built into the two exhaust nozzles in the base of the smoke box. The blowers were used when the locomotive was sitting idle or drifting to maintain a continuous draft through the boiler tubes and up the smoke stacks. When getting underway the steam jets also helped to force the combustion gasses up the stacks until the increasing cylinder exhaust pressure took over. The blower was shut off when running to conserve steam.

The blower line extends from this valve downward below the cab floor, and then turns abruptly to the right side of the locomotive. From this point it parallels the air lines to the lower part of the smoke box where it enters via a nipple. (see the "Boiler, Fire Box, Smoke Box, Super Heater, & Steam Lines" chapter, p.52).

Saturated (Wet) Steam Header (bottom row, 2 valves on right)

Fuel Oil Heater (right side): The first valve supplied saturated steam to the inline fuel oil heater on the right side of the locomotive, just below the cab. It is located on the fuel oil line just before it enters the nozzle into the fire box. It appears that this heater was not used on the 4294.

Fuel Oil Heater (left side): The second valve supplied steam to the fuel oil heater on the left side of the locomotive. This inline heater is located just above the fifth and sixth drivers. It heated the fuel oil prior to entering the firing valve. It was sometimes erroneously called the superheater. This oil heater brought the temperature of the oil up from about 150 to 160 degrees to about 180 degrees.

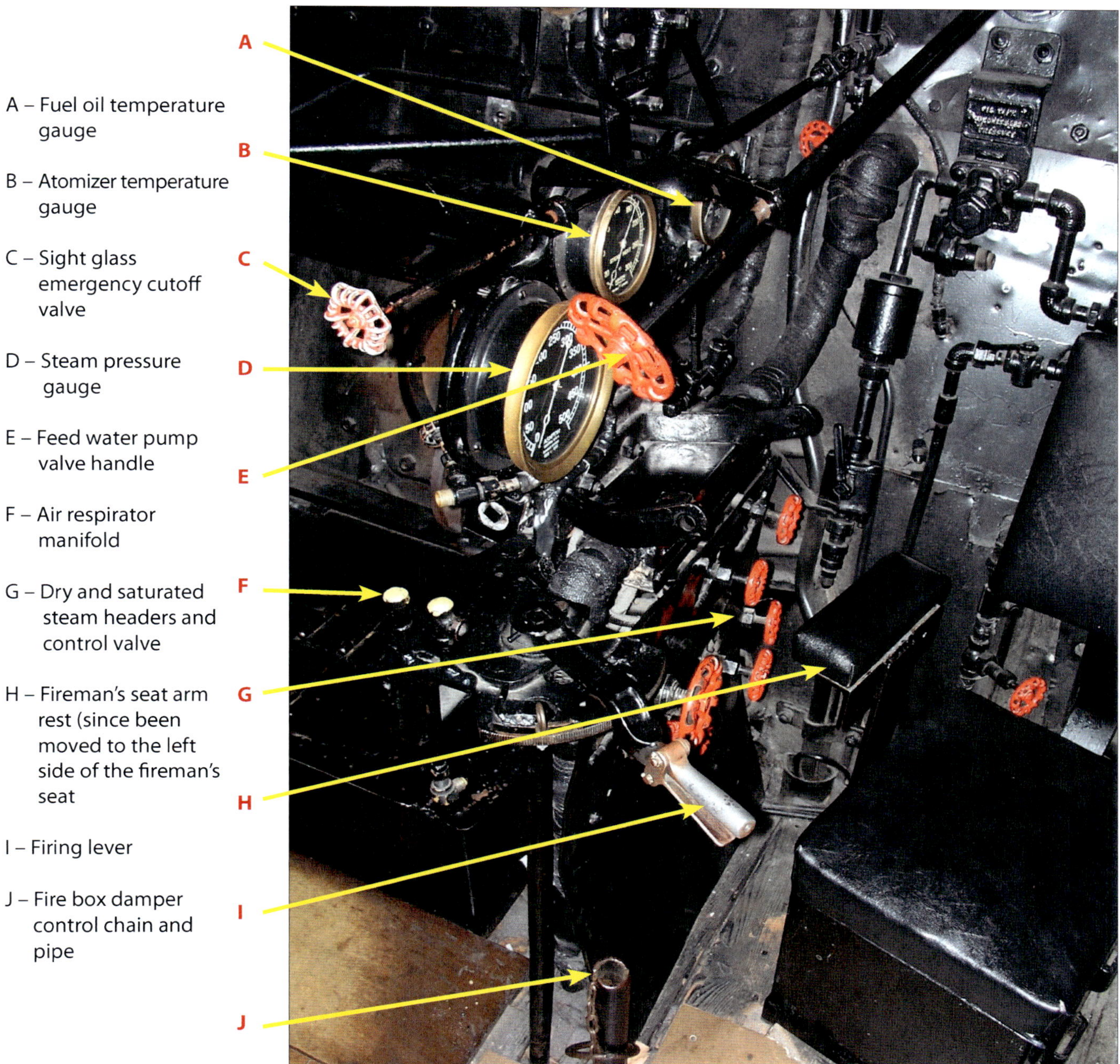

Figure 14 – Fireman's Side Controls

Fuel Oil Heater (tender): The third valve supplied saturated steam to the coil oil heater in the tender. It was used to keep the oil in the fuel oil tank at around 160 degrees. Steam and condensate from this heater was exhausted into the water tank in the tender.

Freeze Prevention: The fourth valve was used to bubble wet steam through the feed water supply line between the tender and the locomotive to keep it from freezing up and bursting in cold weather.

Electric Generator (Dynamo): Wet steam from the turret header was directed into a small turbine that turned the generator. (see "Electric Generator," p.23). The valve handle to operate the generator is located on the control rack that is suspended from the cab ceiling (see Figure 20, p.44).

Fireman's Gauges: There are three gauges just to the right and above the fireman's steam control valves (see Figure 14, p.37). From left to right they are: boiler pressure, atomizer pressure, and temperature of the oil being injected into the fire box (normally approximately 180 degrees).

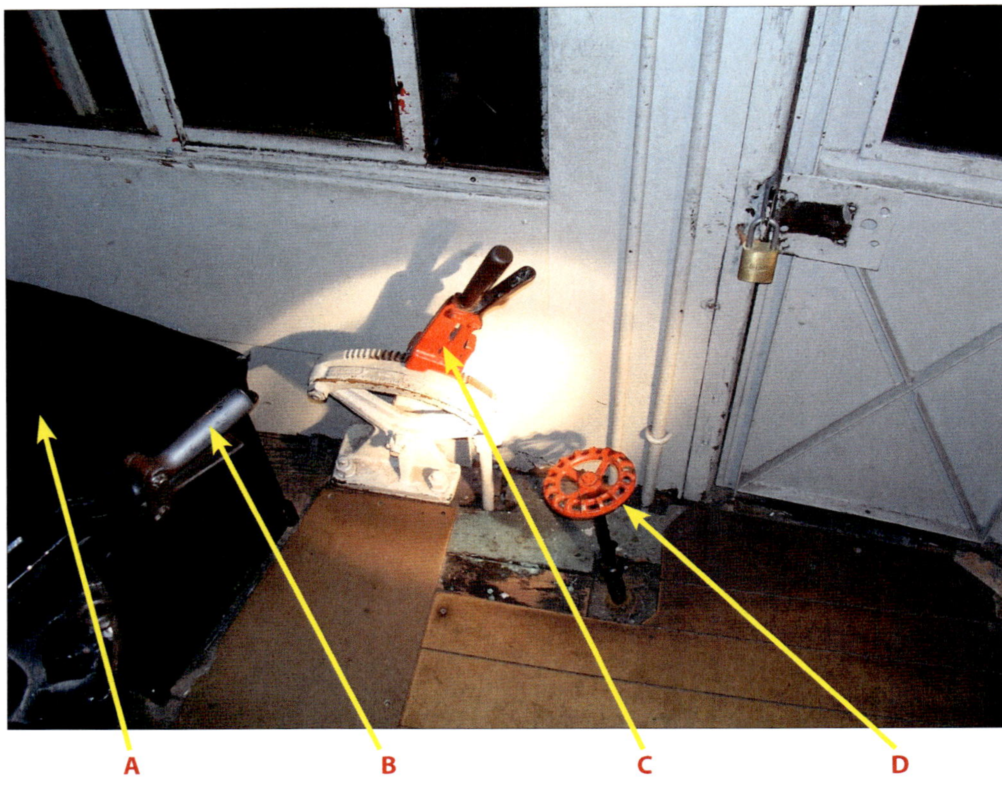

Figure 15 – Fireman's Water Injector Controls

Firing Lever (Fuel Injection Valve): This device is located on the left side of cab, forward and to the right of fireman's seat (see Figure 14, p.37). It was used to control the amount of oil entering the fire box. It includes a horizontal lever and a notched arc or radius for precise settings.

Flag and Tool Holders: On the right side of the cab right below the right front window is a set of flag holders. Red flags were used for emergencies, green to indicate a following section of a train and white to indicate an extra train (one not on the normal schedule).

Fuel Oil Temperature Gauge: This gauge is located on the left side above the fireman's valve console (see Figure 14, p.37). It displayed the temperature of the oil in the tender, which was kept between 150 and 160 degrees (see "Injection Oil Temperature Gauge," p.54).

Gauge Lights (for nighttime running): The lights are missing. They were secured to holes on the flat bent bars that extend in front of gauges.

Headlight Control: The headlight control is located above the window on the fireman's side in a flat metal box about 6 inches across with a lever on its curved bottom. The box is marked with the following positions: off, front dim, front high, back dim, and back high.

Injector Water Valve: Just in front of the injector lever is a large, round, red handle. It supplies water to the injector. It is also a manual overflow check valve which prevented ice from fouling the injector nozzles and thus rupturing the water pipes in freezing cold weather (see Figure 15, p.38). It is just a screw that clamps down on the overflow valve so the injector cannot prime. In freezing weather, when the injector is not in use, the valve was rotated up and steam filled the body of the injector and bled out through the water valve all the way back to the tender.

Metal Box: There is a metal box about 12 inches by 12 inches, with a small window, attached to the front overhead of the cab lining. It contained a first aid kit.

Controls Behind Fireman's Seat

Steam Control to Passenger Cars: The first valve handle on the far left side is attached to a rod that passes through the cab wall to the rear. It is connected to a valve that was used to control the amount of steam that was delivered through an insulated three-inch line to the passenger cars. Saturated steam was delivered to the valve through an insulated line directly from the turret.

Steam To Left Cab Heater: The second valve handle was used to supply steam to the cab heater on the left side of the locomotive.

A – Train indicators

B – Headlight

C – Cooling screen

D – Air horn

E – Stand by marker light holder

F – Nathan injector

G – Blow-down spreader

Figure 16 – Boiler Water Injector

Air Supply To Tender: The third valve handle supplied air pressure to the tender fuel tank, regulated at about five pounds. It is difficult to trace air supply lines to this feature because many have been cut off or disconnected.

Injector Test Valve: The fifth valve is a 1-inch valve fixed with a rubber drain hose. It was used to determine if there was water in the injector, and as an aid in priming this device.

Power Reversing Lever (Walschaert* Valve Gear): This is the large lever located on the right side of cab and just to the front left of engineer's seat (see Figure 7, p.31). It controlled the ALCO Type H Pneumatic Power Reverser which is located on the right side of the locomotive above the forward cylinders. The lever was fitted with a graduated arc or radius (missing on the 4294) which allowed the engineer to select the optimum economic running setting ("company notch"). When this lever was operated it directly controlled the Walschaert gear both on the forward engine and also on the rear engine via a flat bar which runs from the forward engine between the rear drivers to the rear engine gear bar. This bar contains a flex joint. The reverser was called a "Johnson Bar" in smaller, older locomotives and was not power assisted. The front quadrant was used running forward and the back quadrant was used in reverse with neutral in the middle (see "Power Reverser," p.49).

* The *Walschaert* name was spelled with an "s" by the patent owner.

Retainer (tender): Also called a "three-way mountain cock," it is located on the right side of the cab just forward of the engineer's seat, on top of two one-inch pipes that run from the floor to the top of the wall. The tender retainer valve was used to both apply and release the brakes on the tender.

Roof Ventilator: This is a sliding roof hatch that today we would probably call a "Moon Roof" (see Figure 20, p.44). It is a rectangular opening with a sliding cover about 3.5 X 4 feet in size and located in the roof to the rear of the cab. It was operated with a reach rod and a rack and pinion gear with a handle on the fireman's side. It has been mentioned by steam engineers that the vents would always be left open a bit even in cold weather to clear the cab of steam leaking from various valves and fittings.

Record Holders: The government inspection records were kept in several small flat holders above the engineer's window. Some needed to be signed periodically by federal and railroad inspectors.

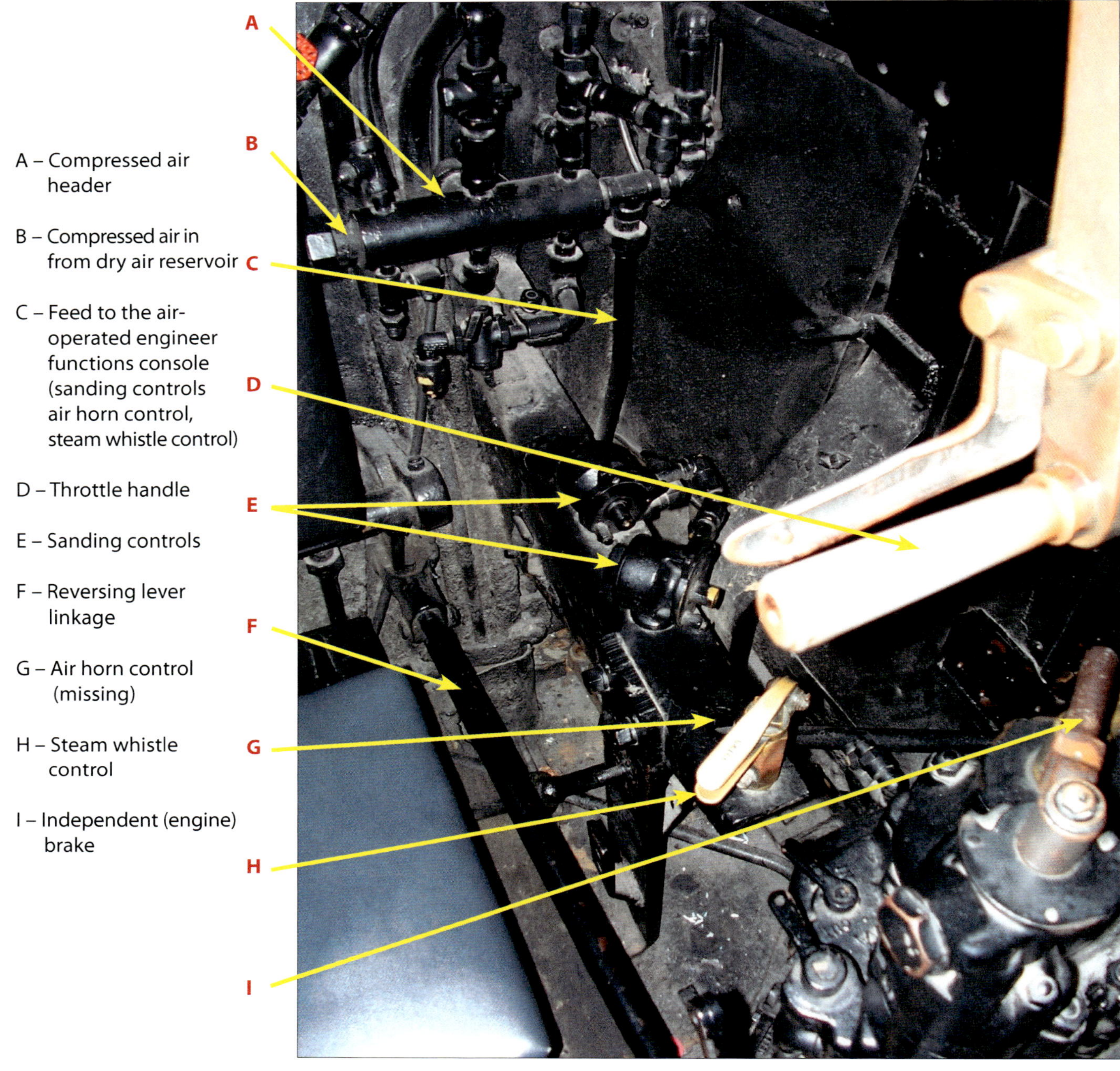

Figure 17 – Engineer's Side Controls

Sand

Sanding Controls: There are two sanding controls, one for each set of drivers (see Figure 17, p.40). Controls were air-operated, and the valves are located to the left and slightly to the rear of the engineer's seat. The control levers are missing. The cab controls operated a set of sand traps for each set of drivers. The sand traps are located just below the sand domes, one on each sand pipe. Note there are sanding pipes for only the first three drivers of each engine on an AC-12. (In contrast, AC-11s had one for every driver.)

Sanding The Tubes: In front of the fire box door is a metal double-door sand box (see Figure 27, p.54). The sand in this box was used to scour the soot out of the boiler tubes. Periodically the fireman would dribble two or three scoops of this sand across the peep hole in the fire box door. The operational draft from the boiler was so strong that it would suck the sand through the tubes and dislodge the soot. After each scoop the fireman would lean out of the cab window and check the color of the smoke. If the smoke was light in color he had removed the soot.

Sand Disposal: The major portion of the sand used to clean the boiler tubes would be blown out of the exhaust stacks. However, a small portion would end up in the bottom of the smoke box and would be cleaned out during scheduled maintenance.

Seats: The engineer's seat is on the right, the fireman's seat is on the left and the front end brakeman's jump seat was on the left front inside wall (note the two bolt holes where this seat was attached). The crew used the under-seat boxes for their lunch pails, grips, tools and supplies.

Signal Pot: The rounded device hanging from the ceiling behind the engineer's seat contained a whistle that was used to communicate to the engineer from the conductor in a passenger car or a snow plow foreman by the use of a code (see "Air Brake and Communication Systems," p.22). When the conductor would make a very brief air application with an air valve in the train, the whistle on the signal pot would sound. The communication was only one way from the conductor to the engineer. Notification codes included:

- 2 whistles = if the train was stopped, "start moving," or If moving, "stop"
- 3 whistles = "back-up"
- 4 whistles = "slow-down"
- 5 whistles = "resume previous speed"

Because air was used to operate the whistles, there had to be a gap between each whistle to avoid any lapse or carry-over.

Steam

Steam Pressure Gauges: The engineer and the fireman each had one. The 4294 operated at 250 psig (1,725 KPa) of steam.

Super-Heated and Saturated Steam: Super-heated (dry) steam was supplied to the cold water pump, feed water pump, air compressors, steam whistle, *fuel atomizer nozzle*, blower valve, tender blow-back lines and main pistons. Saturated (wet) steam was supplied to the electric generator, injector, injector water line freeze protector, cab steam heater, emergency running gear reversing system, operation of cylinder cocks, the oil heater in the tender, passenger cars (for heat), the injector heater cock and the fuel oil heaters on the right and left sides of the locomotive.

Super-Heated (dry) Steam Supply: The super-heated steam supply line header starts from the upper left side of the smoke box (see Figure 28, p.56). The vertical header descends down the left side of the locomotive where it supplies steam to several appliances located at the back of the locomotive. A line also extends forward under the boiler insulation into the cab where it supplies steam to the fireman's dry steam header (see "Fireman's Console Steam Control," p.36).

Saturated (wet) Steam Supply: Saturated steam was supplied from a flanged boiler tap welded directly into the top of the boiler, inside the turret cowling. This arrangement is similar to the nipples tapped or welded directly into the boiler back head for the two water sight glasses. This nipple and valve are not visible because they are inside the turret cowling. Note there is a nipple and valve on the right side of the boiler just below the turret housing. Saturated steam from this nipple is controlled by a reach rod in the cab on the right side, marked "Cylinder Cock." It was used to purge the condensate from the cylinders before starting to move the locomotive.

Saturated steam was also used in the following appliances: electric generator (dynamo), injector, injector waterline freeze protector, cab steam heat system, emergency running gear reversing system, the tender fuel oil heater, and passenger car steam heat. Although there is a Hydrostatic Oiler handle on the overhead appliance rack, the locomotive was never equipped with one.

Speed Indicator in MPH: This Barco speedometer is on the right side of the cab to the left and above the engineer's seat (see Figure 7, p.31). Locomotive speed was measured by an idler wheel located over the third driver on the right side (see Figure 18 below). The idler wheel was turned by direct contact with the driver, and the motion was connected to the speedometer by way of a rotating flexible cable.

Barco Speed Recorder: The speed recorder (see Figure 7, p.31) is a rectangular box on top of the speedometer that contained a paper tape (valve pilot tape) that ran between two reels. A pencil marker, activated by the speed

Figure 18 – Speedometer Linkage (Right Side)

of the locomotive, would leave a continuous record, as the tape moved, showing the locomotive's speed at any given time. The tapes could be reviewed by shop foremen and management to evaluate engineer performance. Motion from the speedometer idler wheel is described in "Speed Indicator in MPH" above. Since the recording device was locked shut, it was sometimes referred to as a "stool pigeon."

Safety Valves: There are three "pop off" valves located in an open steel ring on top of the boiler. The first one pops at 252 psig, the second at 254 psig, and the third popped at 256 psig. There is also a manually operated valve which was used to blow steam directly into the atmosphere during shutdown and to vent the boiler when filling with water. Also, a test gauge was attached to this valve when setting the pop off valves. The pop off valves were set starting with the highest pressure first.

Steam Dome: The steam dome is the highest point of the boiler, located on the center-top of the boiler. It contains the opening of the dry steam pipe. It may have contained a tangential steam dryer installed at the beginning of the dry pipe. This device was designed to spin out any remaining water from the steam before it entered the dry pipe. However, tangential dryers did not work as well as planned and their use was discontinued, and many were removed. It is not known if the 4294 originally had one.

Steam Line to Rear Cylinders: This line runs between the rear set of drivers, from the forward cylinder casting to the rear cylinder casting. It contains two ball joints and two flex joints. The flex joints can be identified by several springs placed around the joints. The rear one is hard to see without the use of a flashlight.

Steam Whistle Control: The brass air valve located to the left of the engineer's seat controlled the steam whistle by operating an air valve near the whistle. There was a second control valve located just behind the steam whistle valve for the air horn. It has been removed.

Super Heater Pyrometer: This gauge indicated the temperature of the super-heated steam. It could also indicate several other problems, including: high water in the boiler, foaming, an inadequate fire, plugged flues, and a defective damper. It is missing, but it was just above the Ashcroft Pilot Valve (see "Valve Pilot Gauge," p.30).

Tender Tank Pressure: Directly behind the fireman's seat is the tender air pressure regulating valve. The air pressure in the oil tank or bunker of the tender was kept at about 5 psig.

Throttle Lever: This lever is located on the right side of the cab, suspended from overhead just to the left of the engineer's seat (see Figure 7, p.31). It is linked to the throttle valve by a

A – Cab ventilator

B – Turret hatch

C – Dynamo (steam-driven electricity generator)

D – Forward sand dome

E – Aft sand dome

F – Passenger steam heat (wet steam)

G – Injector steam (wet)

H – Sanding pipes (6 for each sand dome)

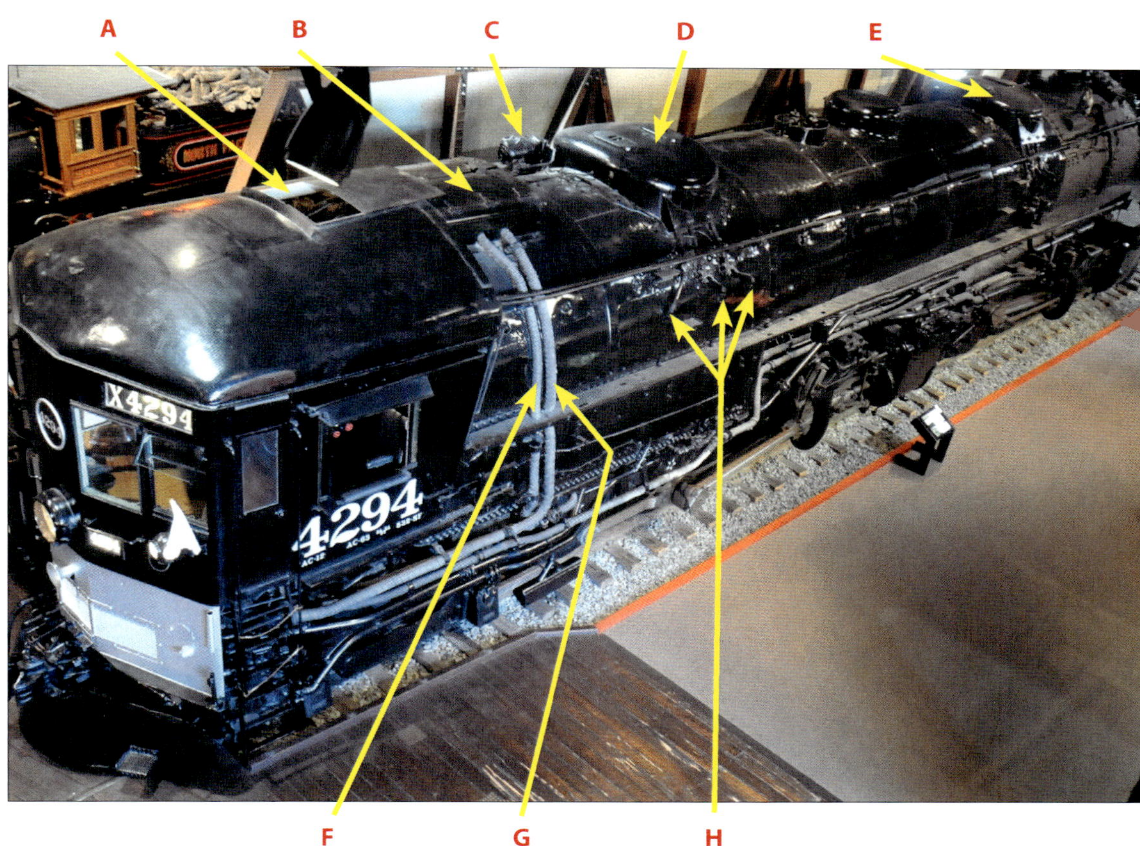

Figure 19 – The Turret

control rod on the right side of the locomotive. The throttle valve is located in the smoke box at the end of the super heater header. It controls the amount of steam from the super heater headers, and ultimately provides super-heated steam entering the valve and main pistons. Note that the control rod has a reversing ("Z") rocker arm, visible on the right side of the boiler that allows the throttle lever to operate in a normal manner like those in a conventional steam locomotive.

Torpedo and Fusee Canister: Track torpedoes were slipped into the slot brackets located on the outside of the round cylinder just to the right of the water cooler (see Figure 10, p.33). They were small, flattened explosive charges held in place on the rails by two bendable metal strips. They were used to signal trains of emergency situations ahead. One torpedo meant caution, two slow and three stop. They were loud enough to be heard above the roar of the locomotive. Fusees (railroad signal flares) were stored inside the canister.

Turret: The turret header is essentially a saturated steam manifold with several valves (sometimes called a "fountain"). It is tapped directly into the top of the boiler. The manifolds and valves are covered with a cowling (the "turret;" see Figure 19, p.43) which is located just behind the cab on top of the boiler. It dispensed saturated steam to various appliances (see "Super-Heated and Saturated Steam," p.41).

Overhead Turret Controls (Valves & Handles): Turret manifold control valves are commonly found on most steam locomotives. The valves are not visible as they are part of the turret manifold, which is described in the previous paragraph. The turret's manifold dispensed only saturated steam to various appliances.

The turret valve handles on the 4294 are described from left to right as follows:

1. **Hydrostatic Lubricator**: There is no hydrostatic lubricator on the 4294. (There is a handle for one which enters the turret, but it is not connected to anything.)

2. **Fireman's Manifold Steam Valve:** This valve provided saturated steam to the fireman's wet steam manifold.

3. **Power Reverser Emergency Valve:** The yellow handle with three arms was used in an emergency to inject steam into the air-operated power reverser system enabling the locomotive to be put into reverse in the event the air brake pressure was lost. This system was required by law. The unique shape of the valve handle made it easier to identify in the dark.

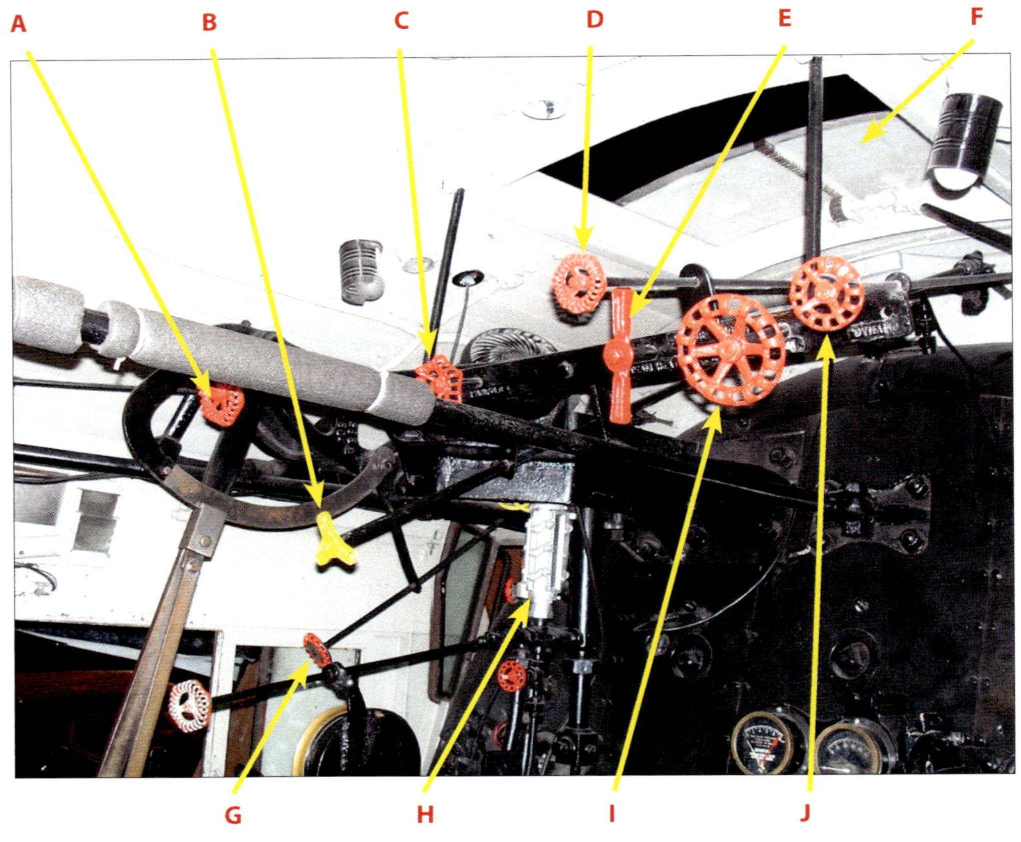

A – Hydrostatic lubricator valve

B – Emergency power reversing handle

C – Steam to oil heater coils in tender

D – Fireman's boiler water sight glass valve

E – External steam supply to passengar car heaters

F – Cab roof ventilator

G – Cylinder flush cock valve

H – Engineer's water sight glass

I – Injector wet steam valve

J – Electicity generator (dynamo) control

Figure 20 – Turret Valve Handles

4. **Water Glass Valve:** This handle, located slightly above the others, controlled the upper shutoff valve on the left side water level sight glass.

5. **Steam Heat Control Valve:** This valve supplied saturated steam to the passenger car heaters.
6. **Injector Steam Valve:** This handle was used to supply saturated steam to the Nathan Type 4000 Water Injector Valve just to the left of the fireman's seat.

7. **Electric Generator Control Valve:** This valve supplied saturated steam to the turbine that powered the electricity generator (dynamo).

Utility Shelf: This is the small shelf and drain below the water cooler (see Figure 10, p.33). It was used to store miscellaneous items as well as draining any water that dripped from the cooler.

Figure 21 – The Turret (with Hatches Open)

A – Dynamo (electric generator)

B – Injector (wet steam)

C – Water glass (fireman)

D – Passenger steam heat

E – Boiler test standpipe

F – Power reverser

G – Wet steam to oil heater coils in tender

H – Hydrostatic lubrictor (not connected)

I – Turret door (left side)

J – Wet Steam header

K – Wet steam boiler tap

L – Wet steam to fireman's header

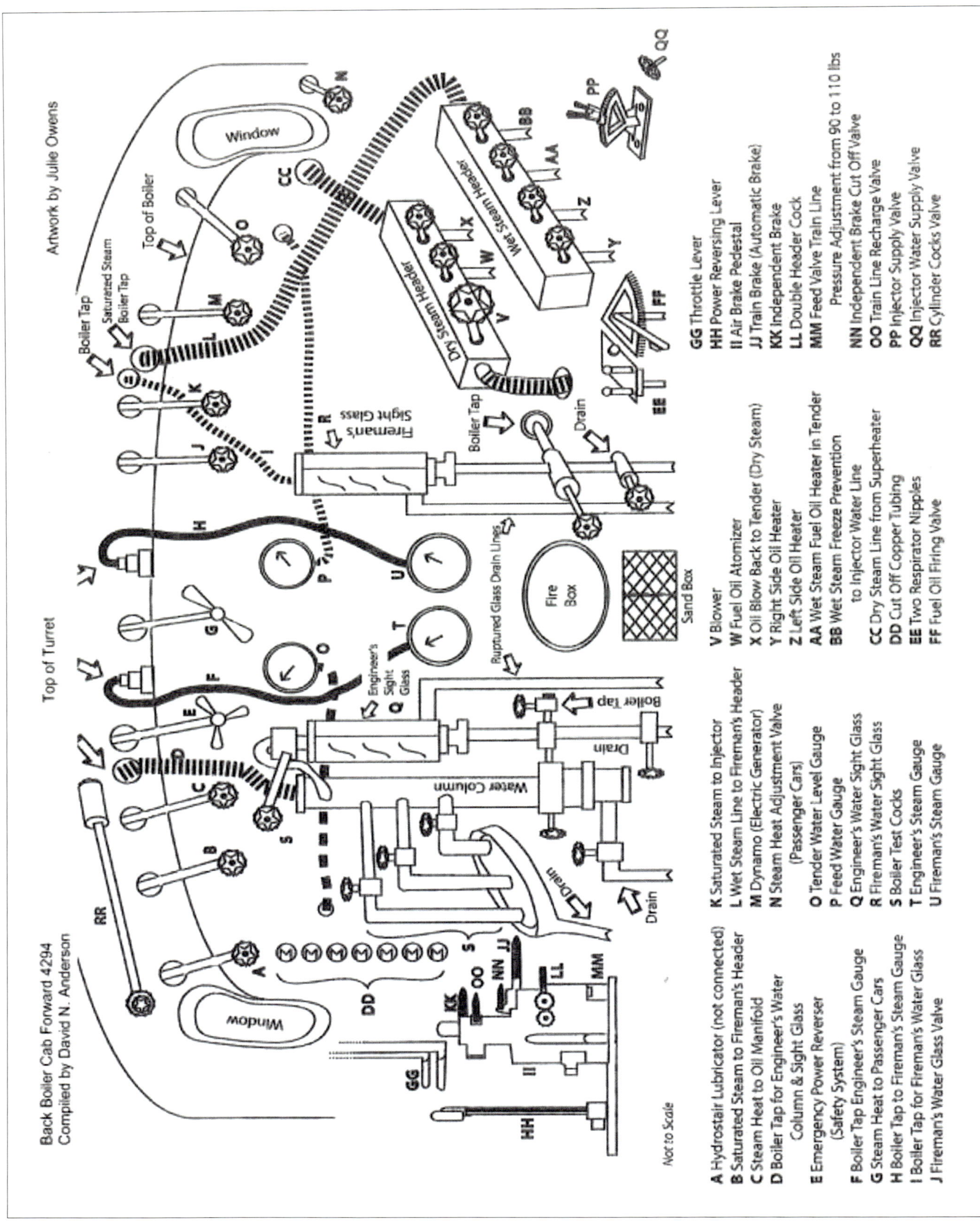

Figure 22 – Boiler Back Head Features

7: Running Gear (The Engines)

A – Typical piping flex joint

B – Star indicates internal bearing and denotes type of axle lubrication

C – Brake shoe (cast iron)

D – Boxpok-style driving wheel

Figure 23 – Articulation Piping Flex Joints

Articulation: The wheel base of the 4294 is so long that it precluded the use of a single rigid frame as it would be unable to negotiate tight curves. Constructing a flexible connector between the two engines solved the curve problem but created a myriad of other problems. Everything that passed from the rigid boiler and front engine to the rear engine had to be done with flexible connections (referred to as "flex joints"). This aspect created both design and maintenance problems.

Bearings: Both trucks and the drive wheels have bronze and/or Babbitt metal friction bearings with spring loaded lubricators. A bronze bearing arch is placed above each axle and lubricated with a felt pad which was pressed against the bottom of the axle by a cloth-covered spring. Oil is delivered to the pads through a wicking process from the oil reservoir in the lower part of the journal boxes. The journal boxes on the locomotive trucks and the tender are located on the ends of the axles. The bearings and journal boxes for the drivers are located in special niches in the cast frames.

Note: At the time the 4294 was built, roller bearings were expensive and in short supply, which was one of the reasons they were not installed on Cab-forwards.

Tin Lubricant: On some bearings a groove was created around the middle and filled with copper or tin. The reason for this was if the bronze bearing for some reason began to wear rapidly and heat up, the copper or tin, each having a lower melting point, would melt and act as a lubricant to keep the axle from being scored.

Castings (Frames): There are two on every cab-forward. The frames were cast in one piece with integral features to hold various components. The one piece casting also included all cylinder housings, apertures, nooks, raised holders and notches for various locomotive components such as bearings, appliances, piping, air reservoir tanks etc. Cast frames are much stronger and far more rugged then the previously used bolted or welded frames. They were manufactured for Baldwin by General Steel Castings Corporation. The length and weight of these two castings are phenomenal.

Draw Bar (Engine): The two engines are coupled with a single U-shaped draw bar located just behind the front saddle casting. Its forward (curved) end is secured to the front engine with a 7-inch diameter articulation pin that allows lateral movement. It is emplaced from below and held in place with a metal bar. The connection to the rear engine is with two 4½-inch pins which are placed horizontally on each end of the U-shaped coupling. This configuration allows for vertical movement of the trailing engine. This articulation design allowed AC locomotives to negotiate curves of up to 18 degrees. (see item "S" in Figure 40, p.69). This coupling is illuminated on the 4294 with a light.

The visible side of the coupling looks like an "I" beam. The 4½-inch cap on the left side horizontal pin is visible behind the fifth driver.

Draw Bars (Tender): The locomotive is connected to the tender with two parallel draw bars (see Figure 36, p.65). They are visible from the left side of the locomotive. The upper one is the main bar and the lower is the safety bar.

Drive Rods: The locomotive drive rods are made of steel with the engine number and "front" or "back" and "right" or "left" markings stamped into each rod. They were numbered by Baldwin as if the engine would run in the opposite (conventional) direction. They were polished so cracks could be more easily detected when they were magna fluxed. This was done every time the rods were removed. If a rod survived the magna flux test a small green star was painted on it. None of the green stars survived the cleaning and polishing before the locomotive was placed in the museum. All of the drive rod bearings are fitted with pressure grease fittings.

Side Rods: Side rods connect all of the driving wheels. They are made of the same steel as the drive rods.

Rod Pin Bearings: All of the drive rod and side rod pin bearings are friction type and made of bronze. The actual bearings are bronze inserts that were fitted between the driver opening and the pin. They generally were cut lengthwise into three equal pieces and lubrication holes were drilled through them. The bearing caps have lubrication fittings and were lubricated with grease. They were called floating bearings, thus they were set up to basically run in only one direction. Engineers were forbidden to run a cab-forward in reverse at more than 25 mph.

Drive Wheels: Each engine has eight 63-inch diameter Boxpok drive wheels. The axles are fitted with Franklin spring loaded drive box bearing lubricators fitted into the engine frame inboard of the wheels. They were also known as spring pad oilers or lubricators. The lube oil containers are equipped with a sight glass for easy inspection of the oil levels. Bearing lubricators were inspected after every trip by engine house personnel from a pit below the hot locomotive. The stars painted on the drive wheel centers indicate this type of lubrication system (see Figure 23, p.47 for an example of a Boxpok drive wheel).

Drive Wheel Casting: There was some question on how the Boxpok drive wheels were cast as they are not solid and have an opening between the massive spoke-like members. The wheels were cast in one piece. One side of the mold was placed horizontally on the casting floor and a sand casting, called a "core," of slightly cemented sand in the shape of the interior part of the wheel was placed on it. It was then covered with the second side of the wheel mold. Once the molten metal was poured and the casting process completed both sides of the mold were removed. The next task was to remove the slightly cemented interior sand core by manually digging it out of the middle of the wheel. It is assumed that the reason for an open wheel was to increase its cooling capacity.

Drive Wheel Water Sprayers: Above each driver can be found a water spray nozzle. During heavy downhill breaking, the friction between the tires and the cast iron break shoes would generate a tremendous amount of heat. Some of this heat could be dissipated by spraying water on the drivers. The tender wheels are also equipped with a similar set of sprayers. The location of the control valve in the cab was just behind the two sanding valves on the engineer's side. The sprayer over the seventh driver on the left side is missing. Often when running downhill the engineer would bypass the engine brakes and only use the train brakes in order to prevent the tires from over-heating. During heavy braking, freight trains would sometimes stop a while to allow the brakes to cool.

Lateral Motion Boxes: The fourth and fifth drivers were fitted with lateral driving boxes (ALCO Lateral Monitoring Cushioning Devices). This allowed the drivers to move a short distance laterally lessening the pressure on the rails. They are fixed with two springs and a bronze pressure plate on each to lessen wear on the journal boxes during turns. They are not visible from the sides of the locomotive.

Lubricators

Flange Lubricators: Flange lubricators were/are located on the first and fifth drivers and the front truck (see Figure 24, p.49). The front truck lubricator is an open can and valve type. There is one on each side. The flange lubricators on the first and fifth drivers have been removed. The brackets that held then in place are still there just above and a little back of the vertical center line of the drivers.

Rear Truck Lubricator: The pivot bearing on the rear truck is lubricated with an open can and valve arrangement like those on the front truck.

Lubricating Pumps: Each of the two engines was fitted with two Nathan mechanical lubricating pumps, one on each side. They are installed on top of the guide yokes (see "Yokes," p.51). The pumps on the left side were used to lube the cross heads and related moving valve gear and piston mechanisms. The pumps on the right side were used to lube the drive wheel bearing journal boxes. The lubricators were powered by an eccentric rod connected to the curved links on each engine. There is a rotating ratchet in each oiler that automatically apportioned set amounts of oil to various engine bearings and sliders. The lubricator on the left side of the rear engine is missing. Also missing on almost all of the lubricators are the copper tubes and rubber hoses that carried the lube oil to the various mechanical parts.

Figure 24 – Flange Lubricator

Cylinders

Main Cylinders and Pistons: There are two for each engine – four total. Each one is 24 inches in diameter and has a piston stroke of 32 inches. Note the 4½-inch steel piston rods (See Figure 39, p.68).

Drift Relief Valves: Each set of cylinders is fitted with a set of drift relief valves. They were designed to prevent a vacuum in the cylinders when the engine was drifting downhill and thus prevent the drawing of dirt and sand into the cylinders from the fire box. They are located on top of the valve cylinders and would automatically operate when drifting. When drifting, the engineer would apply a little steam just to keep the pistons lubricated.
Note: The drive mechanism on the AC was reciprocating. Power was generated on both the forward and backward stroke of the pistons.

Valve Cylinders: There are also two of these for each engine – four total. They are 11 inches in diameter and located atop the main cylinders. The piston stroke was controlled by the Walschaert valve gear which was set at the Baldwin Locomotive Works when the locomotive was manufactured. The valve piston was set to supply steam to the main piston for a maximum of 81.6 % of its stroke.

Saddle Castings: A part of the main casting (frame) that carries the weight of the cross heads. After the casting was poured the cylinders had to be machined and numerous bolt holes drilled and threaded (see "Castings (Frames)," p.47).

Cross Head "Alligator Type": The cross heads are the heavy sliding mechanisms on the ends of the main piston rods. They slide in heavy, rugged bars to resist the heavy angular forces on the main rod connection to the main pin on the drive wheel. They are located just forward of the valve pistons. The cross head bearings are made of steel covered with a flat sheet of tin that is covered with Babbitt. They were lubricated through copper tubing from the Nathan mechanical lubricators on the left side of the engine. They are supported by the guide yokes.

Power Reverser: An ALCO Type H Pneumatic Reverser is located on the right side of the locomotive (see Figure 25 below). It is a 2-foot long cylinder activated by linkage from the reversing lever in the cab. It operates the Walschaert valve gear, which controls the direction of the locomotive through the movement of the radius rod. This rod also adjusted the stroke of the valve pistons which optimizes the most efficient use of the steam. Adjustment of the valve cylinder stroke was known as "adjusting the cut-off." It could also be operated with saturated steam in an emergency (see "Walschaert Valve Gear," p.69).
Operating Note: The geometry of the two engines and the articulation joint were basically set up for the locomotive to go forward. Because of this, any reverse operation was limited to 25 mph.

A – Pneumatic power reverser cylinder

B – Blower line

C – Train pipe line

D – Mechanical lubricating pump

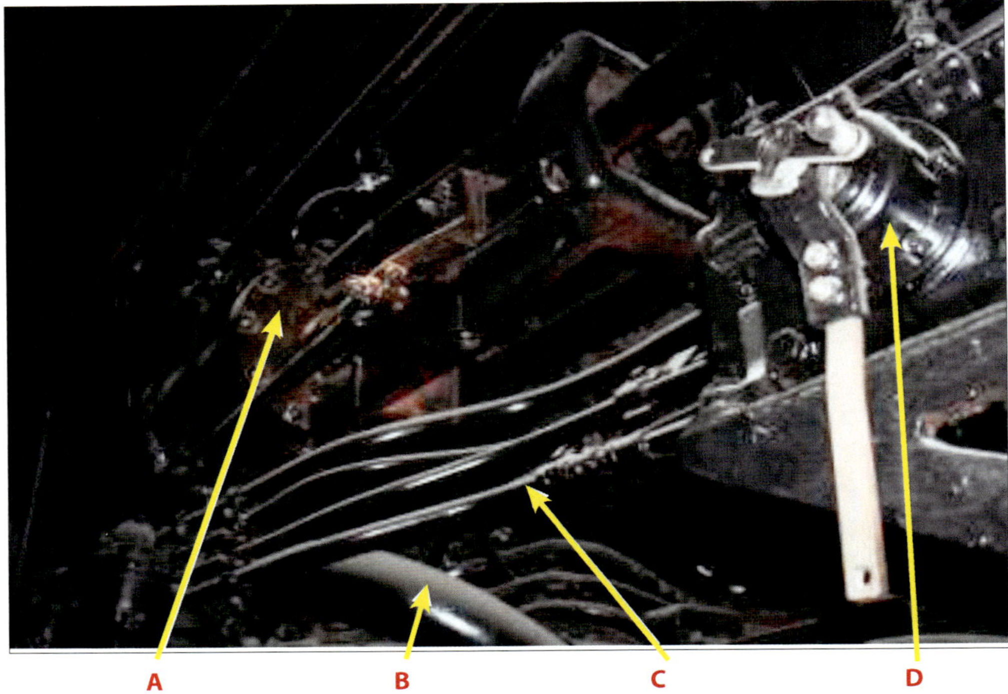

Figure 25 – Pneumatic Power Reverser Cylinder

Sliding Waist Bearer Plate: The aft weight of the boiler over the articulated engine was carried on a brass slip plate which is just above the space between the second and third drivers of the rear engine. It is visible from the left side of the locomotive. Note the 8 in. pipe above the slip plate. It contains two opposing springs that aided the rear engine in swinging back to the center after coming out of a curve. The lubrication for this slip plate probably came from one of the lubricating pumps on the left side of the locomotive (see "Lubricating Pumps," p.48).

Tires (Driver): Tires on the driver wheels (see Figure 18, p.42) are made of steel, however not all were turned to the same diameter, albeit the differences were very small. It has been noted that after installation some were scored opposite the pin on the wheel with a line and opposite a line on the tire with a punch mark, which, if found to be offset, would indicate that the tire had slipped on the wheel. (see "Tire Retaining Safety Clips," p.51). A set of these marks has been found on the left side of the locomotive adjacent to the pin on the 5th driver.

Turning Tires: Due to the many curves and excessive brake applications in the Sierra, tires had to be machined (peeled) every six weeks or when needed. The engine was placed on a special Lidgerwood track, fitted on one end with a cable reel. The cable reel was used to pull the engine across a section of track during which the peeling operation would take place. All of the drivers would be peeled (trued) at the same time.

The process involved three types of steel cutters called "peelers" which were bolted onto the brake beams that held the brake shoes. The engine was pulled along the track with the cutters being engaged by air brake pressure. The first pass would true up the tread of the tire, the second pass would redevelop the flange, and the third pass would finish both the tread and the flange.

Occasionally an extra hard flat spot would be found. This was caused by the heat generated by skidding during a break application. Because it was harder than the rest of the wheel this spot would have to be ground off with a hand grinder. It would take a day to peel all of the drivers.

Changing Tires: The tires were changed out when needed, or at every annual over-haul taking from 7 to 10 days to accomplish. The engine would be backed up on a wedge which compressed the springs over a set of drivers taking the weight off of the axle. After the springs were compressed and blocked, the driver set was moved over a three ft. removable gap in the track. The tire was heated through the use of a circular pipe with the same diameter as the tires. It was perforated with several holes through which gas flame jets were directed onto the tire until it expanded. It took about 20 minutes to expand. Once expanded, the tires could be hammered off from a pit below. Replacement tires were installed hot and as they cooled they would shrink onto the drive wheel. Replacement tires, when cold, were usually a smaller diameter than the wheel. Sometimes shims would have to be used to make a tight fit.

As an alternative method, a locomotive was placed over a drop pit, the springs on a set of drivers were compressed and the driver set was lowered into the pit. From there it was moved laterally, brought to the main shop floor level where the tires were replaced. The CSRM has a drop pit in the shops.

Tire Retaining Safety Clips: Note the five 3-inch steel tabs or clips welded across the interface between the tires and the drive wheels (see Figure 18, p.42). They are intended to hold a tire on the wheel if it became loose due to heat expansion during heavy braking. They are welded on and must be cut off during tire replacement.

Trucks: The leading truck is a two-axle Commonwealth type. The early 2-6-6-2 Cab-forwards built prior to 1913 had a single-axle Hodges front truck. After an accident SP converted them to a two-axle truck to improve the tracking of the first set of drivers. This feature was also used to help carry the weight of the firebox. The trailing truck is a single-axle Commonwealth type, as shown in Figure 36, p.65.

Wheels and Accessories

Driver Brake Shoes: The brake shoes are made of cast iron. Brake shoes were replaced by removing the old shoes from the brake adjustment mechanisms, called cams, below the back of each set of drivers and adding new shoes. This work was done from a pit below the track.

Drive Wheel Lubricators: The painted star on the driver axles (see Figure 23, p.47) indicated that they were lubricated with oil spring pads. The pads are located in a bearing box between the wheel and the notched casting. Also there was a ½-inch rubber hose oil line to each of the driver bearings boxes from the Nathan lubricating pumps on the right side of the locomotive.

Speed Indicator Wheel: This device is located just above the second driver on right side of the engine. It consists of a rubber-tired wheel, the recorder, and a set of springs that hold it tight against the top of the driver. It is connected to the speed indicator in the cab by a linked chain in a flexible housing (see Figure 18, p.42).

Counter Balanced Drivers: Starting with the AC-7s (1937) and after, cab-forwards had better balanced drivers, called "Boxpok" drive wheels (see Figure 23, p.47). The counter balance weights on the drivers were cast with more precision. They also were cast with several 1-inch holes in the balance weights. This allowed the emplacement of heaver metals to help in the balancing. Thus engines could run at higher speeds with less vibration and bouncing. The maximum safe speed of the later ACs was rated at 65 mph; however, speeds were usually kept below 50 to 55 mph. The nominal speed of these units was about 30 mph. A harmonic motion would occur at about 45 mph, but this action would cease as speed was increased.

Yokes (Guide Yoke): The guide yokes are the large, curved, vertical metal castings that support the Walschaert valve gear slider cross head guides, the main head guides and the end of the drive rods (see Chapter 12, p.68). There are two yokes on each engine, one on each side. They also provided a place on top for the Nathan lubricating pumps.

Above: SP 4191 near Madeline, California, June 27, 1955. Don Ball collection.

8: Boiler, Fire Box, Smoke Box, Superheater, and Steam Lines

Blow-off (Blow-down) Apparatus: Just behind the cab on each side of the locomotive is a lever which, when activated by the fireman or engineer, would blow the sediment out of the mud ring at the bottom of the boiler. The precipitate (gunk) would be discharged through the blow-down spreaders located just outboard of the tracks on each side of the locomotive (see Figure 3, p.24 and Figure 26 below). If this sediment was not regularly removed it could cause foaming or scaling in the boiler or in the boiler tubes and an excessive use of water. Sediments are brought into the boiler with water in the form of dissolved solids. The quality of the water at the numerous water sites varied considerably. Under normal conditions the boiler was blown down every three hours. Some ACs were equipped with an automatic blow-off system; however, the system on the 4294 is manually operated (see "Boiler Blow-down Spreaders," p. 23).

A – Blow-down control lever (outside and behind cab, one on each side

B – Fire box

C – Blow-down spreader

D – Front truck

Figure 26 – Blow-Down Spreader

Boiler

Boiler Check Valves: On the left side of the boiler, above the rear engine, are two check valves. Both are used to put water into the boiler. The front valve delivers water from the injector, and the rear one delivers water from the feed pump. Note that they are placed above the level of the tubes in the boiler. If placed above the tube level, the buildup of scale on the tubes is less than if placed level with or below the tops of the tubes. Most railroads painted them red.

Boiler Anchors: There are four places where the boiler is fastened to the castings (engine frames). The first one is at the front of the firebox (sometimes called the foundation ring), the second one is between the 2nd and 3rd drivers and the third one is at the end of the forward saddle casting. The fourth anchor is located between the 6th and 7th drivers on the rear casting. This one is a sliding waist bearing plate which allows the back section of the boiler to slide laterally over the casting when the locomotive is going through a curve. A part of this sliding attachment is a transverse tube located above the sliding plate. It contains a left and a right spring that help the engine to move back to center when exiting the curve. These springs are not visible.

Boiler Drop Plugs: There are six drop plugs located on top of the crown sheet (the top of the fire box). Drop plugs were made of brass or another metals with a lesser melting point than the boiler crown sheet. This configuration allowed the rapid entry of water into the fire box to extinguish the fire. Brass plugs with a small, fast melting metal core were not as fast in putting out the fire. The use of drop plugs was very successful. There were over 120 instances where they prevented boiler explosions.

Boiler Jacket: The jacket includes a 4-inch thick sheath of insulation made of asbestos-magnesia which is covered with a sheet of metal.

Boiler Tubes and Flues: There are a total of 331 22-foot long tubes and flues in the boiler. Of those, 91 are flue tubes, each 3½ inches inside diameter (ID), and the remaining 240 are boiler tubes, each 2½ inches ID. The tubes are on the periphery of the tube bundle and the flues are in the center (see Figure 29, p.57).

Engine Start Up: The start up the locomotive from a cold boiler was accomplished by the following steps:

1. The boiler was filled with warm water by connecting a hose (house line) to the 2-inch pipe opening built into the blow-down "Y" on the lower left corner of the fire box.
2. The vent valve on top of the boiler was opened.
3. When the boiler was filled with water to the proper level, the vent and the fill pipe were closed.
4. Superheated steam was fed into the locomotive from a stationary boiler in the round house, or from a nearby locomotive, through a 1-inch pipe fixed with a nipple on the left side located just above the first driver. If steam was unavailable compressed air could be used. Once the steam pipe was connected, dry steam could be introduced into the system by opening a valve on this pipe located a few inches in from the nipple.
5. Once supplied with steam, or compressed air, the blower, the fuel oil atomizer and other dry steam driven appliances could be activated.
6. Next, the congealed oil in the fuel oil line from the tender was purged back into the tender using the tender blow-back valve on the fireman's manifold (see Figure 13, p.36).
7. The initial ignition was done by tossing ignited waste into the fire box through the fire box door in the cab until the oil finally started burning.
8. Hot oil was sprayed into the fire box through the fire box atomizer and it would flash into flame.
9. The blower was turned on.
10. When it was determined that the oil fire was successfully burning, the fire box door was shut and the safety bar was tightened. Hot oil, sprayed forcefully into the fire box through the fire box atomizer nozzle, kept the fire burning. The fire box door was never opened again until the locomotive was returned to a shop or other service location.

It would take about four hours to get the steam pressure up to 250 lbs. If possible, the time was extended to better allow various metal parts of the boiler to heat up slowly, thereby reducing the possibility of stress cracking. Because of the problems caused by the expansion and contraction of metal, once fired up, engines were generally kept hot until a routine monthly boiler inspection and washings, or when they had to be shopped.

Boiler Stay-bolts: Stay-bolts, made of wrought iron, suspend the fire box within the boiler housing. Those in non-critical locations have a hollow core and would indicate leakage if they became cracked. They were called "tell-tale" bolts. The bolts suspending the combustion chamber just behind the fire box are flexible stay-bolts. They were installed in a two-inch nipple with an exterior plug which, when removed, reveals a rounded bolt head with a slot which could be turned to adjust the mechanical spacing between the combustion chamber and the top or side of the boiler. Round-head stay-bolts were necessary in certain parts of the fire box and boiler because of the excessive expansion during locomotive startup.

Boiler Washer Nipples: Just below the hand rail, at the level of the crown sheet, and in other parts of the boiler, are fitted several 2½-inch washout nipples with plugs. When plugs were removed it would, allow the cleaning of the water legs (annulus) area around the lower part of the fire box with high pressure water sprayers. Scale and sludge would be washed down to the mud ring where it was drained through the 2½- inch drains at the bottom of the boiler. A deposit of scale 1/8-inch thick on the outside of the fire box could reduce its efficiency by 15 percent.

Boiler Water Capacity: The boiler could hold about 10,935 gallons of water.

Boiler Fire Box Light Shield: During WWII thin metal plates were installed on both sides of the locomotive to shield the glare of the fire box from hostile ships at sea when the locomotive was traveling along the coast. One of these shields can be seen just above the gap between the front truck and the first driver.

Waist Plates: There is a flexible waist bearer plate supporting the back of the boiler. It is made of heavy sheet metal (see "Sliding Waist Bearer Plates," p.50).

Density Light: A light is installed just to the right of the smoke stacks allowing the fireman to check the density of the smoke at night (see Figure 30, p.58; see also "Density Light," p.23). If the color of the smoke was a gray haze the fire was just right.

Exhaust Stack Temperature: The exhaust temperature from the locomotive smoke stacks was approximately 450 degrees.

Feed Pump Exhaust Line: On the left side of the engine is a 2-inch line which originates at the lower, forward part of the smoke box about 1 foot above the bottom. It is attached to the boiler as it extends forward to just above the forward cylinders where it is directed downward alongside, then to the bottom center of the left cylinders to a point just above the tracks. This pipe is open-ended and has no valves. It is the feed pump water heater exhaust line. It disposed of the air that was freed from the water as it was being heated. This exhaust line was placed on the left side so the fireman could get a visual check on the

Figure 27 – Fire Box

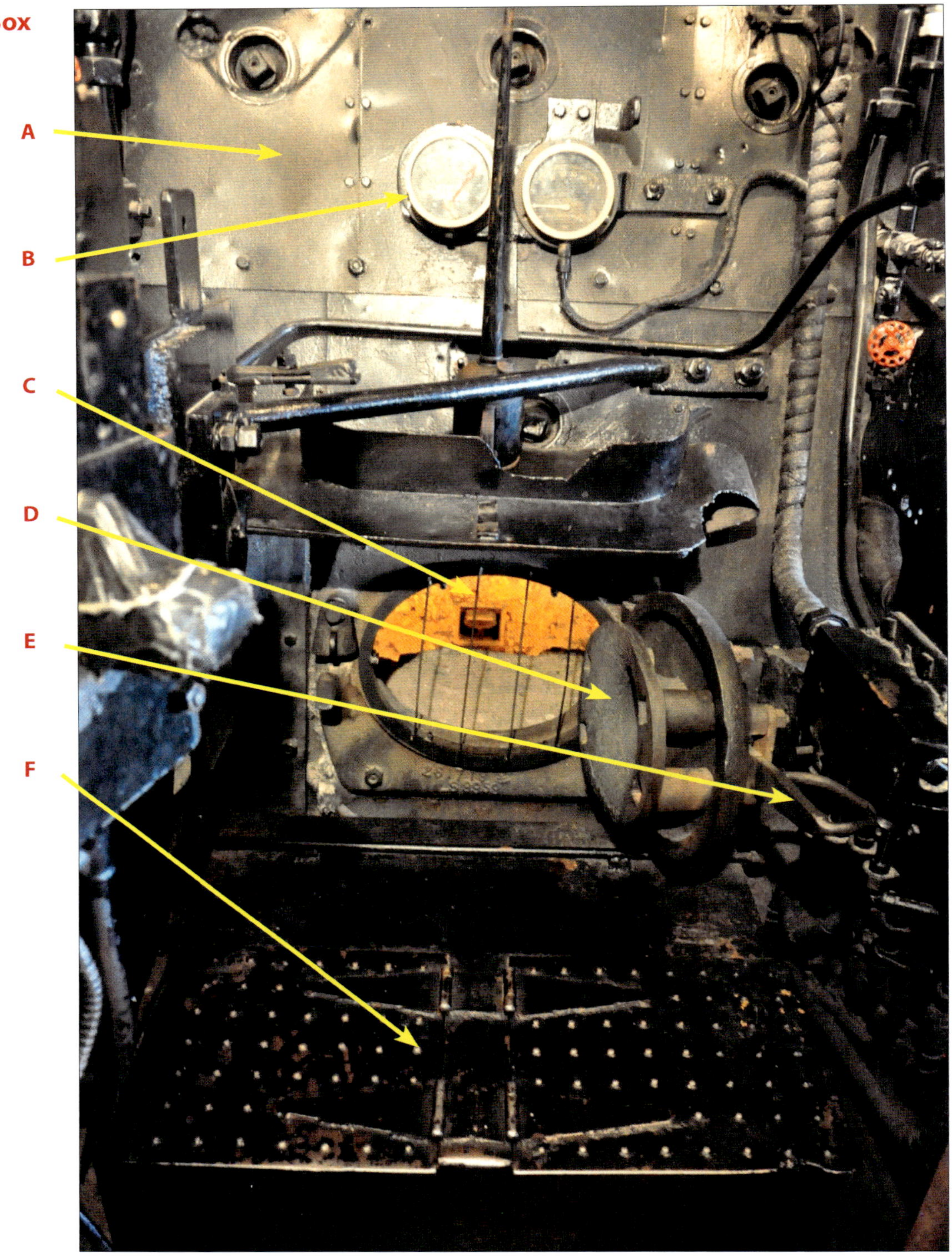

A – Back head

B – Tender water tank lever indicator

C – Fire box interior

D – Fire box door

E – Fire box door latch

F – Sand box doors

status of the pump.

Fuel Injection Atomizer: On the lower back inside wall of the fire box is a square hole about 16 inches by 16 inches. In the middle of this hole is an elliptical Von Borden (oil atomizing) nozzle through which fuel oil was sprayed into the fire box (see “Fuel Oil Atomizer Nozzle,” p.41). The nozzle is fitted with a steam entry port several inches before the opening into the fire box. With this configuration the superheated steam atomized the oil as it was injected into the fire box. The steam both heated the oil and atomized it. As the atomized oil was injected into the fire box it would flash into flame before it reached the opposite wall, which is partially lined with fire brick. After flashing the flame would curl back over itself, into the combustion chamber and pass through the boiler tubes into the smoke box.

Fuel Oil Injection Temperature: Fuel oil injected into the fire box was about 180 degrees Fahrenheit. When a locomotive was steamed up, super-heated steam was used to vaporize the oil as it was injected into the fire box.

Injection Oil Temperature Gauge: The fuel injection atomizer is fitted with a temperature sensor and a cable with a woven covering. This cable extends from the sensor, which is implanted in the atomizing nozzle, to a temperature gauge just to the right of the fireman's seat (see Figure 14, p.37).

Fire Box Lining: The lower half of the fire box is lined with fire brick. The upper half was left unlined because more than 50 percent of the heat was transferred from the top of the fire box. Every roundhouse had a worker called a brick man who repaired fire box lining at overhauls. He was a part of the boiler maker crew.

Fire Box Damper: The primary fire box damper is a flap about 8 inches by 2½ feet located at the lower forward edge of the fire box. It is controlled with a chain which runs through a 2-inch steel pipe located just to the right and forward of the fireman's seat (see Figure 14, p.37). The pipe has two slots in its lip which links of the chain can be slipped into to adjust and secure the opening of the damper. The cab end of the chain is fitted with a ring about 4 inches in diameter to prevent it from slipping entirely into the pipe (see "Fire Box Air Damper Control," p. 35).
Note that there are automatic secondary dampers on each side of the firebox, below the mud ring. They are fixed with counter balance weights. Air was sucked in as needed. They are not visible because they are hidden inside of dust protectors. The protectors are half cylinders about 3 feet long.

Flex Joints: There are a set of exterior ball and flex type pipe connections on each side of the locomotive where it is articulated. There are also two ball and two flex joints on the main steam line between the forward saddle casting and rear saddle casting, which runs between the rear drivers. The forward ball joint is in the forward engine casting and the rear ball joint is in a housing which is a part of the rear casting. The flex joints are hard to see and they were harder to work on. It was said that the smallest man in the crew would have to squeeze in there if these joints needed to be tightened. The flex joints can be identified by the presence of several coiled springs.
Forward Engine Exhaust Lines: Just below the steam lines to the forward saddle castings are large uninsulated exhaust pipes. They extend on an upward slope from the forward cylinders back to the smoke box, one on each side of the locomotive (see Figure 28, p.56).

Rear Engine Exhaust Line: This single line extends from the center of the rear casting just in front of the cylinders to the bottom of the smoke box. The exhaust from the rear engine first passes through an expansion joint just in front of the rear saddle casting, then through a Franklin Radial connection before it enters the bottom of the smoke box. The radial connection (swivel) was necessary because the rear engine is articulated and therefore moves laterally with respect to the front engine.

Sanding the Tubes: While operating, the boiler tubes would have to be periodically sanded to remove the buildup of soot that, if left unchecked, could reduce the efficient operation of the locomotive. The operational draft through the boiler tubes was so strong that the fireman needed only to dribble the sand above the peep hole in the fire box door and it would be sucked in as it fell. It would take two to three applications to clear the tubes. To check on the effectiveness of the sanding the fireman would hang out of the cab window and look at the smoke. The sand box is located just below the fire box door (see Figure 27, p.54; see also "Sanding the Tubes," p.41).

Sand Disposal: Almost all of the sand used to clean the boiler tubes would be ejected with the exhaust from the smoke stacks. However, the remainder would end up on the bottom of the smoke box and would be cleaned out during scheduled maintenance (see also "Sand Disposal," p.41).

Smoke Box Drain: There is a 6-inch drain on the bottom of the smoke box. It extends downward then a short distance to the right side. The total length is about 1 foot. It is closed with a 6-inch screw cap which is fixed with a short piece of steel welded across it to make it easier to remove. This drain was used during heavy maintenance for cleaning of the smoke box.

Steam Features

Steam Supply Point (Round House Steam): There is a 1-inch pipe extending from the left side of the locomotive just above the first driver and a two inch line extending from the front of the cab that could be used to deliver start up dry steam to the locomotive while in a round house or shop. Steam, hot water, and air were normally available at most round house stalls.

Dry Pipe: The dry pipe is the steam supply line that extends internally from the steam dome to the super heater header in the smoke box. The throttle valve is located at the end of the super heater headers, not at the opening of the dry pipe in the steam dome. This configuration insured a quicker response when the throttle valve was opened.

A – Dry steam line
B – Dry steam source
C – Dry steam whistle
D – Exhaust splitter
E – Smoke stacks (under the splitter, one for each engine)
F – Feed water heater
G – Smoke box
H – Front engine steam line
I – Front engine exhaust line
J – Feed water line to boiler check valve
K – Builder's plate
L – Smoke box drain line
M – Water supply line to the feed pump
N – Steam line to feed water pump
O – Feed water pump

Figure 28 – Smoke Box Side

Steam Pressure: The boiler operating pressure was 250 psi. During scheduled maintenance the boilers would be tested at 25 psi above this operating pressure. Until the AC-4s in 1928, the boiler operating pressure on the ACs was 210 psi.

Steam Dome: The steam dome is the highest point of the boiler and is located on the center top of boiler. It contains the opening of the dry pipe. It may have contained a tangential steam dryer at the beginning of the dry pipe. This device was designed to spin out any entrained water from the steam before it entered the dry pipe. However, the tangential dryers did not work as well as planned and they were discontinued, and many were removed. It is not known if the 4294 had one.

Safety Valves: There are three pop-off (safety) valves located in an open steel ring on top of the boiler. The first one pops at 252 psig. The second at 254 psig, and the third popped at 256 psig. There is also a manually operated valve, which was used to blow steam directly to the atmosphere during shut down or to vent the boiler during filling. The pop-off valves were set starting with the highest pressure first.

Main Steam Supply Lines: The main steam lines extend from the throttle valve on the super heater header in the smoke box to the front cylinders on both sides of the locomotive. They are the larger insulated pipes that slope downward to the front saddle casting.

Smoke Color: Under normal operations the color of the smoke from the stacks was a light gray. At night it was difficult to see the color of the smoke even with the light near the stack. Experienced firemen could determine a proper fire by observing the color of the glow through the peep hole.

Steam Line to Rear Cylinders: This line runs between the rear set of drivers from the forward saddle casting to the rear saddle casting. It contains two ball and two flex joints. The flex joints can be identified by several springs placed around the joints. The rear one is hard to see without the use of a flashlight (see "Flex Joints," p.55).

Steam Temperatures: Saturated steam was about 400 degrees and super-heated steam was a little above 700 degrees.

Super Heater: The 4294 is equipped with an Elesco Type-E super heater. A U-tube type superheater could produce superheated steam at about 700 degrees. *Superheating did not increase the boiler pressure; rather, it increased the steam temperature before it entered the pistons.* Superheating could increase the efficiency of the locomotive by 35 percent.

Super heaters had many maintenance problems, most of which were due to the impurities in the water at many of the water stops. The installation of tangential steam dryers (see "Tangential Steam Dryer" below) was supposed to have eliminated most of the scaling in the super heater tubes, but this was not the case on the 4294. It is believed that this locomotive was never equipped with a tangential steam dryer.

Tangential Steam Dryer: Tangential steam dryers were installed in the steam domes at the start of the dry pipe in some of the ACs. This steam driven device was designed to swirl any water out of the saturated steam before it entered the dry pipe (see "Steam Dome," p.26).

Thermic Siphons: They were funnel-shaped tubes installed in the boilers and were intended to increase water circulation to minimize hot spots that would lessen the contraction and expansion stress on the fire box sheets. It is believed that they were not installed on the 4294.

Throttle: The American Multi-Valve Smoke Box throttle is controlled by linkage from the cab and is located at the end of the super heater header (manifold) in the smoke box. The throttle linkage has a reversing joint (Compensating Lever-"Z" rocker) attached to the outside of the boiler jacket about half way back to the smoke box on the right side. This reversing rocker caused the throttle to operate in a conventional manner, i.e. pull back to go forward and push ahead to stop. This rocker also prevented premature opening of the throttle valve during startup (see "Throttle Lever," p.42).

Figure 29 – Boiler Tube Sheet

9: Brake System

Brake System Westinghouse (8-ET): The brake system is made up of several components, including: the two air compressors, the main air reservoir, the secondary reservoir, the air filters, the brake pedestal (LA-PC), the feed valves M-3-A and M-3, the double heading cock, the two duplex air gauges, the distributing valve, brake cylinders, the train signal system and several other components.

Air Pressure: Air pressure on SP freight trains was maintained at 90 psi. Passenger trains maintained 110 psi. The different pressures could be set by a valve on the side of the air brake pedestal (See Figure 6, p.29).

Air Compressors: There are two reciprocating Westinghouse Cross Compound 8½-inch air compressors located on the back of the smoke box. Originally they were installed on the right side of the boiler, but starting with the AC-6s they were installed on the end of the smoke box. They exhausted directly into the atmosphere, rather than the smokebox, giving Cab-forwards a distinct sound like "pew-pew, pew-pew...." They could be heard while standing, running, or especially when drifting downhill. The air compressors have built-in lubricators with a quart-size F-3 lubricator on each pump (see Figure 30 above).

Air Hoses and Angle Cocks: There are two air hoses dangling from the front of the locomotive and two on the rear of the tender. The larger hose is connected to the 1¼-inch train line (pipe), and the smaller one is connected to the 1-inch signal pipe. The angle cocks (valves) at the front of the locomotive are found just above the leading wheel on the front truck on the right side of the locomotive. On the tender, the angle cock for the train line is located just below the back edge of the tender, and the one for the signal pipe is located up underneath the back of the tender.

Air Pressure Governor: This device (located between the two air compressors) was set to maintain a constant pressure in the main (wet) air reservoir. The M-3-A Feed Valve, located on the Brake Stand, maintained the pressure in the secondary (dry) reservoir at either 90 or 110 psi, depending on how it was set.

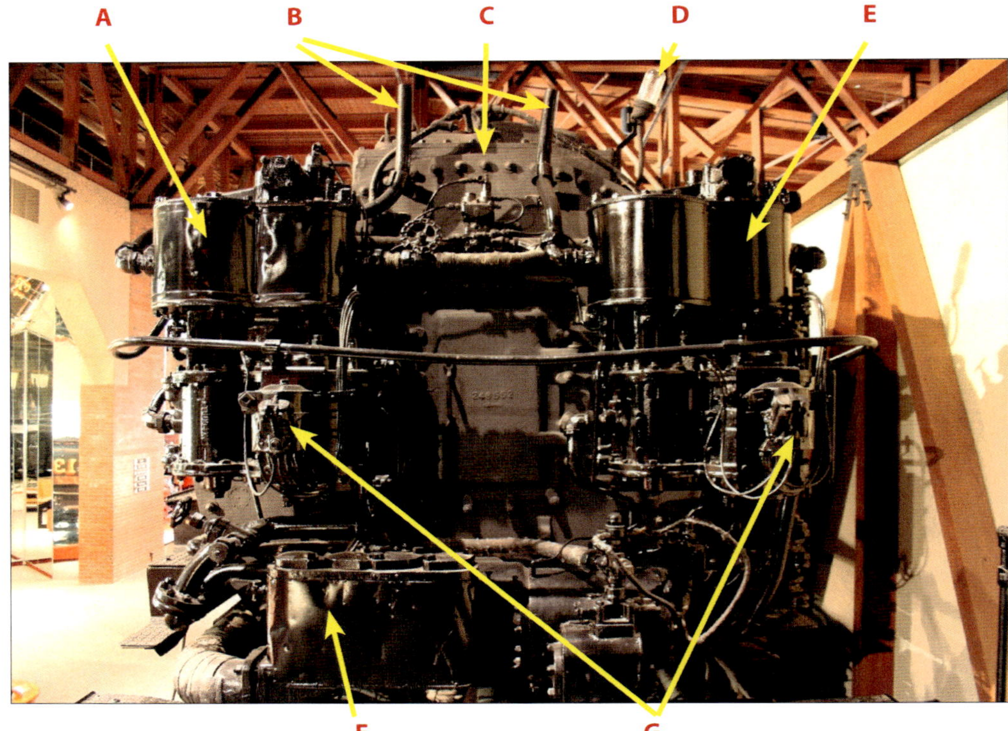

Figure 30 – Smoke Box End

Air Reservoirs

Main Air Reservoir (Wet): The main (wet) compressed air reservoir is the large tank under the cab floor (see Figure 31 on the following page). Air from the two air compressors on the end of the smoke box is pumped through two 3-inch lines, then directly into this reservoir. From the main reservoir air passes through the inter air cooler, then through a water knockout, a filter and finally into the secondary (dry) reservoir.

A – Secondary air reservoir (dry)

B – Air lines from compressors

C – Main air reservoir (wet)

Figure 31 – Air Reservoir (Right Side)

Inter Air Cooler: This device consists of a coil of one inch pipe located behind the screen on the front of the cab (see Figure 2, p.22). It was used to cool the air from the main wet reservoir in order to drop out any accumulated water before the air entered the main dry reservoir. Incidental water in the brake system, if frozen, could clog the train line and cause serious trouble during heavy braking.

Secondary Air Reservoir (Dry): The secondary (dry) reservoir is smaller (about 2/3 the size of the main reservoir), and is located just behind the main (wet) reservoir (see Figure 31 above). It supplies air for the air brake system, the cab air respirators and several appliances.

Cab Controls

Brake Pedestal (Stand): The brake pedestal 8-ET (LA-PC) is located just to the left and in front of the engineer's seat (see Figure 6, p.29). On the side of the pedestal, near the floor level, are two air feed valves. The top valve, an M3A, regulated the pressure in the train line (pipe) to 110 psi for passenger or 90 psi for freight trains. The lower valve, an M3, reduced the pressure in the main dry reservoir for the independent brake and the signal system to about 45 psi.

Train Brake Control Handle (Automatic Brake): This long handled control is located near the top of the pedestal. It controlled the brakes on the entire train. Note the small handle just below the main brake handle. It was used to partially recharge the air in the train line to release the brakes when getting underway after a stop. In an emergency the train brake was pushed to the far right. This would vent the air in the train line and apply the brakes on the entire train. While running, the train brake handle was in the far left position.

Independent Brake Control Handle: This control is located above, and is smaller than, the train brake. It was used to cut off the locomotive brakes when running downhill to prevent over heating of the locomotive brake shoes and wheels. It was also used to stop the locomotive when it was not connected to a train or when it was pulling only a few cars. Note the small valve handle just below the independent brake handle. It was used to cut the system off when the locomotive was pulling a train. This system operated on about 45 psi of air pressure.

Doubling Heading Cock: This valve is located on the front of the brake stand. It consists of two partially geared wheels. One is fitted with a handle. When double heading, the activation of this valve would cut the locomotive brakes totally out of the train brake system. The cock is open with the handle down, and closed with the handle up, parallel to the pedestal.

Tender Brake Retainer Valve: Just to front left of the engineer's seat and against the cab wall are two tall pipes with a brake retainer at the top. It was used to both set and release the brakes on the tender. It was required by law.

Air Pressure Gauges: The air reservoir pressure gauge set

Figure 32 – Right Side Piping

(also called the “Quadraplex” gauge) is located on the left side and forward of the engineer’s seat (see Figure 7, p.31). It is the rectangular box containing two gauges with two pressure indicators (needles) on each gauge. The red needle in the left gauge showed the pressure in the locomotive brake cylinders; the black needle showed the pressure in the train line. The right hand gauge showed the pressures in the two air reservoirs. The Quadraplex gauge was missing when the locomotive was donated to the museum, but another one, along with its light fixtures, was donated in 2005 and promptly installed.

Brake Pipe Vent Valve: This HP-4 vent valve is located above the gap between the third and fourth drivers on the right side of the locomotive. This device was used to insure quick action during a cab or train brake application.

Train Line (Pipe): The 1¼-inch inside diameter train line (pipe) is on the right side of the locomotive. It is paralleled by the 1-inch inside diameter signal pipe. The train line segment on each car is connected to the next car through a rubber hose with a metal connection called a “glad hand” (see Figure 2, p.22), fitted with a rubber bushing. Each of the two rubber hoses on the locomotive has a different size glad hand and each type of glad hands has a different sized rubber gasket. Although they are different in size they could in an emergency be connected to bypass a car.

Distributing Valve: The 8-A air distributing valve can be seen above the second and third drivers on the right side. When activated, the device: (1) permitted air to flow into the locomotive brake cylinders, (2) maintained any desired air pressure in the brake cylinders, and (3) permitted air pressure to exhaust from the brake cylinders. It was also used to disconnect the locomotive and tender from the train air brake system to keep the locomotive and tender wheels from overheating.

Brake Shoes: There is a brake shoe adjacent to the back of every driver, as well as on all of the tender wheels. (see Figure 23, p.47). The shoes are made of cast iron. There is a 6-inch adjustment on the travel of the brake cylinder piston. The railroad liked to keep the adjustment at about three inches, but four inches were allowed if an engine was needed for a run. Note that when it was decided to permanently reverse the direction of the locomotive, the braking lever assembly on the drivers and the tender wheels had to be re-engineered to place the brake shoes on the back side of the drive and tender wheels.

Brake Cylinders: There are two UAD brake cylinders for each engine (set of drivers). The cylinder on the left side of the forward engine is located between the 3rd and 4th drivers, and the cylinder on the left side of the rear engine is between the 5th and 6th drivers. Likewise, the cylinder on the right side of the forward engine is between the 3rd and 4th drivers, and the cylinder on the right side of the rear engine is between the 5th and 6th drivers. All of the cylinders are mounted vertically. They all can be seen with some difficulty using a flashlight.

Above: Overhead view of the 'monkey deck' between locomotive and tender. (Boyd Reyes photo)

Below: Another perspective of the monkey deck between locomotive and tender. (Boyd Reyes photo)

Brake Cylinders (Tender): There are two brake cylinders on the tender. They are located between the trucks and are visible from the left side. The locomotive and the tender are both part of the same brake system.

Equalizing and Reduction Limiting Reservoir: This reservoir is located on the left side of the locomotive between the second and third drivers.

10: Appliances

A – Train line (pipe)

B – Cold water pump

C – Rear engine casting

Figure 33 – Cold Water Pump (Right Side)

Feed Water Equipment: The Worthington feed water heater units were installed starting with AC-4s, and they were updated to Type 6 on the AC-6s. They consisted of the following three components:

Cold Water Pump (Feed Water Heater Supply Pump): A cold water pump was used to transfer water from the tender to the feed water heater (see Figure 33 above). It was powered by a steam turbine. This device is located under the monkey deck on the right side of the locomotive just forward of the trailing truck. The flexible cold water hose from the pump to the feed water heater makes a large loop on the right side of the locomotive. This hose is reinforced with an imbedded metal coil. The steam line to the turbine is also on the right side but it just has a simple flex joint.

Cold Water Feed Line: On the right side of the locomotive just over the rear engine is the cold water feed line from the tender. It cannot be missed because of its large curve. The curve is essentially a flex joint.

Feed Water Heater: Worthington Type A6 Feed Water Heater system is installed inside the back of the smoke box (see Figure 30, p.58). It was used to preheat water before it entered the feed water pump. The rectangular hump on top of the smoke box just behind the exhaust stacks is part of this device (see Figure 28, p.56). Part of the exhaust steam from the two engines was directed into the feed water heater. Spent steam from the cylinders was sprayed through two nozzles to heat the water.

Feed Water Pump: A Worthington Type SA feed water pump is located below the air pumps on the back of the boiler just above the monkey deck (see Figure 30, p.58). It features a steam driven reciprocating pump which put water directly into the boiler through a check valve on the left side of the engine just above the 6th driver. It was only used when the locomotive was in motion. When the engine was standing, the water could not be adequately preheated as there was no exhaust steam, and adding cold water to a hot boiler was discouraged. Thus when the engine was not underway, water was added to the boiler using the injector. It delivered water to the boiler at about 240 degrees. The feed water pump has a built-in lubricator.

Feed Pump Exhaust Line: On the left side of the smoke box a little above the bottom is a 2-inch line that is tapped into the feed water pump heater. It extends forward then downward and ends just below the front left side cylinders. It permits the escape of air which separates from water when it is heated. The outlet is placed so that the fireman can observe the discharge (see "Feed Pump Exhaust Line," p.53 for details).

Note: The feed water system included water transfer from the tender, heating and injection into the boiler. This entire process was controlled by the notched handle just to the right and slightly above the fireman's seat (see Figure 4, p.25). The notch in the handle was used by the fireman as a reference point indicating the position of the last application. The feed pump also contains a drift control valve. When steam pressure to the cylinders got below 50 psi the feed pump system would automatically shut off, and it would restart when the pressure reached 50 psi. The feed water heating system could increase the efficiency of the locomotive by 10 to 20 percent.

Injector

Water Injector: A Nathan Type 400 Non-Lifting Injector is located just behind the cab ladder on fireman's side (see Figure 16, p.39). It had no moving parts. The venturi tube that was located up into the bottom of the injector has been removed. The bottom plate has also been removed and is now alongside the engineer's seat. This device could be used while the locomotive was at rest or in operation because the steam used to operate it would pre-heat the water. Water was injected into the boiler through a check valve on the left side of the locomotive above the space between the 5th and 6th drivers. It was important that only hot water be injected into an operating boiler to lessen the possibility of stress cracking. Southern Pacific often painted the injector and the boiler check valves red. This was not done when the engine was repainted for museum display. The injector had a capacity of 7,000 to 12,000 gallons per hour. Cab-forward firemen used the full volume from the feed pump when running. Any adjustments in the supply of water to the boiler would be made with the injector.

Injector Water Supply Valve: A standard steam locomotive feature, it supplies water to the injector. The valve handle (see Figure 9, p.33 and Figure 15, p.38), when totally activated, clamped down on the overflow valve so the injector could not prime. When the overflow valve was engaged, steam filled the body of the injector and bled out through the water valve all the way back to the tender. This prevented freezing in cold weather. The valve had to be closed when the injector was not in use as it was a non-lifting injector placed way below the tender water level. If it was not closed water would be wasted.

Injector Lever: The injector lever (painted red) is located on the left side of the cab just forward of the fireman's seat (see Figure 15, p.38). It was used to inject steam and water through a venturi, forcing water into the boiler. Saturated steam is supplied to the injector from the fireman's control console (see Figure 13, p.36).

Above: Roundhouse mechanic adding alemite to the linking rods of SP 4216 at Colton Yard on February 5, 1954. Chard Walker Photo, Pacific Railroad Society Archive Collection.

11: Tender

A – Passenger train steam line

B – Monkey deck

C – Three axle truck

D – Fuel oil tank

E – Journal box

F – Water tank

Figure 34 – Tender Side View

AC-11 Class Rectangular Model 220-R-5: 22,000 gallon rectangular tenders were first used on Class AC-7 locomotives in 1936. The model tender preserved on display with SP 4294 is number 9357, which was built with AC-11 No. 4262 in March, 1943. These two engines swapped tenders in 1955 and the original was scrapped.

Bottom Frame: The tender's bottom frame casting was made for Baldwin by General Steel Castings Corporation.

Brake Cylinders: There are two (one for each truck) located between the trucks. They are both visible from the left side of the tender.

Chafing Plate: The connection between the tender and the engine was always kept tight with a constant-pressure chafing-plate (see Figure 35, p.65). This device is visible from each side of the tender.

Coupler Draw Bars: The tender was connected to the engine by two draw bars (see Figure 36, p.65). The top bar is the main bar, and the bottom bar is the safety bar. They are visible from both sides of the locomotive.

Fire Hose and Reel: It is known that AC-12 Class 220-R-6 tenders were equipped with a fire hose and a reel on the front deck. If there was one on the 4262 tender it was probably mounted on the front deck.

Fuel Oil: The fuel oil used was Bunker C, a heavy grade, low gravity, very viscous oil with a high BTU value. It had to be heated to about 150 to 160 degrees to get it to flow. A maximum temperature of 160 degrees was maintained because at any higher temperature there was the possibility of gas bubbles occurring in the line to the cab which would cause an irregular flow of oil through the nozzle. When the oil was sprayed into the fire box it was around 180 degrees. The last 20 degrees of temperature was gained from the inline oil super heaters and the dry steam used to spray the oil into the fire box.

Fuel Oil Capacity: The upper front tank on the tender held 6,100 gallons of Bunker C oil. It was kept at a temperature of 150 to 160 degrees (see Figure 34 above). The oil tank (bunker) is outlined by the diagonal row of tightly spaced rivets on the side of the tender. It contained enough fuel to run an AC from Sacramento to Sparks, Nevada (Reno) and back, although it was always topped it off at Sparks

Fuel Oil Tank Pressure: The fuel oil tank was pressurized at 5 psig. A reducing valve is attached to the vertical pipe on top of the tender. This valve was used to set and maintain the necessary pressure in the oil tank. This pressure moved the oil forward to the cab and to the fire box injection nozzle without the need for a pump. The valve that supplied the oil tank with air is just behind the fireman's seat. Oil tank pressure was also necessary to move oil to the fire box from a half-empty tank when the locomotive was travelling uphill.

A – Steam heat line to oil tank

B – Coupler draw bar

C – Signal hose

D – Chafing plate

E – Locomotive rear truck

Figure 35 – Tender Chafing Plate

A – Left main cylinder of rear engine

B – Rear frame casting

C – Rear truck

D – Steam line to passenger cars

E – Water line to the locomotive

F – Main draw bar

G – Safety draw bar

Figure 36 – Tender Coupler Draw Bars

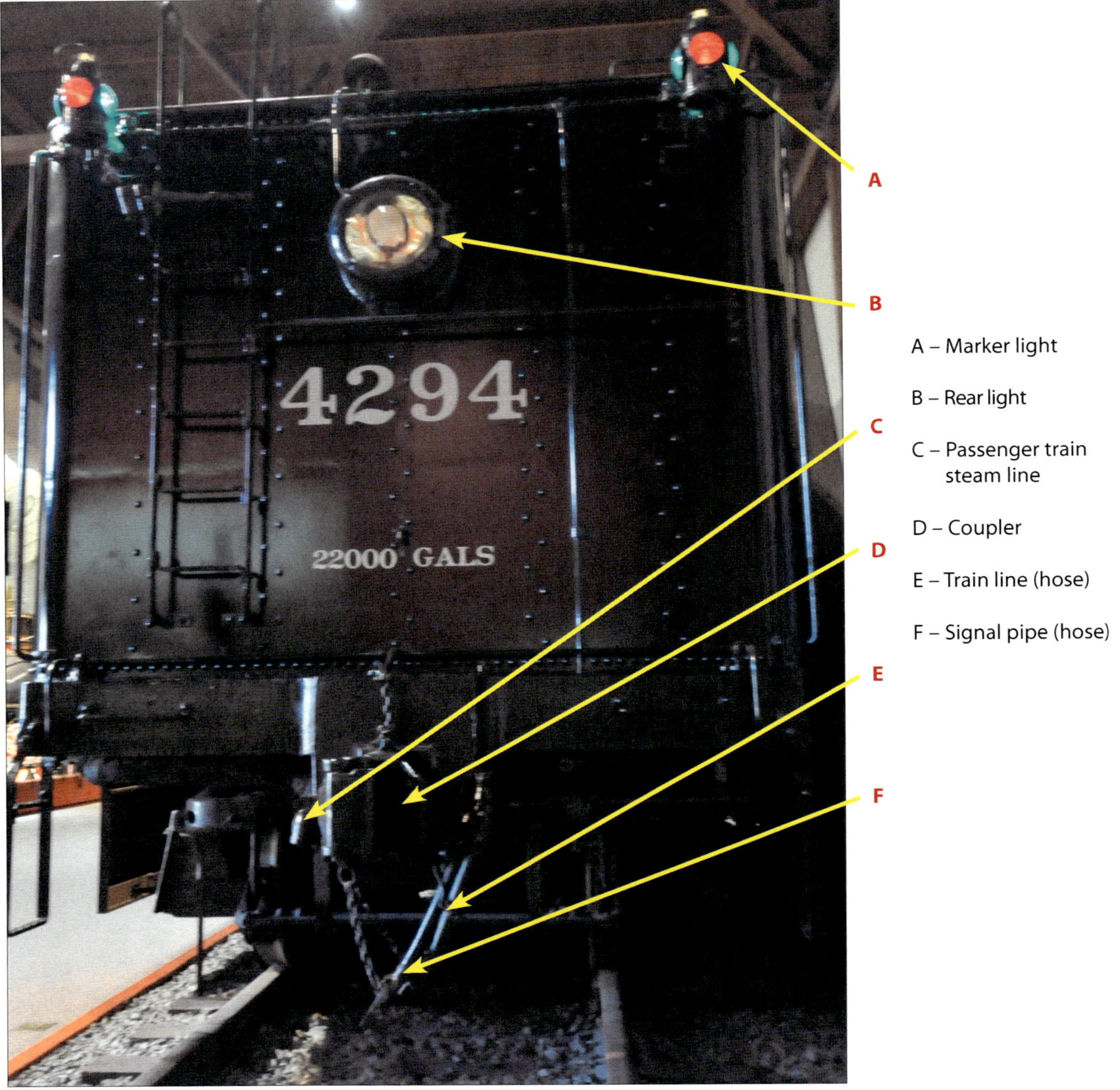

Figure 37 – Tender Rear View

Gauging Rod: This is a metal rod with volume markings that was kept on top of the tender. It was inserted in an opening on the top of the tender oil bunker to determine the amount of oil remaining. The pressure on the oil tank had to be relieved prior to using the gauging rod.

Water Capacity: The water capacity of the tender was 22,000 gallons. The amount of water in the tender could be determined with the tender water level indicator gauge on the back head of the boiler (see Figure 12, p.35), or visually by opening the forward manhole and counting the number of internal ladder rungs that were exposed. Sometimes this task was done by the front end brakeman. The total tender capacity (the 22,000 gallons of water, plus the oil capacity of 6,100 gallons) is about equal to the volume of two suburban swimming pools.

Water Fill Hatches (Manholes): There are four manhole covers on top of the tender, which made it easier for the engineer to spot the locomotive at the water columns. The fireman could

Figure 38 – Tie Sprayers

open the manhole cover closest to the water column spout.

Water Quality: Water quality was usually a problem. The water quality in the tender was maintained, if appropriate, by tossing in several Nalco brown colored balls (nicknamed "meat balls") consisting of neutralizing chemicals. This practice did not always work: Probably depending on the dissolved solids in the water, sometimes the balls would not completely dissolve and would partially block the intake pipe to the locomotive.

Oil Heater Lines: A 1½-inch hot wet steam pipe extending from the locomotive to the forward end of the tender just below the oil tank was used to heat the bunker oil in the tender before start up and during operation. The tank heater is a coil type. Waste water from the heating coil passed through a steam trap and was diverted into the tender water tank; it was not wasted.

Passenger Train Steam Line ACs were regularly assigned to pull passenger trains over the Sierra and other heavy grades. Therefore many of these engines were fitted with a passenger train steam line for heating the cars. It is the insulated line coming out of the turret and along the left side of the locomotive, then under the left side of the tender. It is also visible at rear of the tender (see Figure 37).

Retainer (tender): On the right side of the cab, just forward of the engineer's seat, are two one-inch pipes that run from the floor to the top of the wall. On top of the pipes is a car air brake retainer valve (three-way mountain cock; see p.39). The tender retainer was needed to control the brake system of the tender when running downhill.

Trucks: The tender is supported by two, three-axle, articulated Buckeye trucks with 36-inch wheels. Each truck has a 10 foot wheel-base. They are 3,500 lb. lighter than the previously-used Commonwealth type trucks.

Tie Sprayers: At about the center of, and underneath the tender, just above the rails on each side, is a set of sprayers (see Figure 38 above). The sprayer supply pipes are tapped right into the bottom of the tender. They were used to wet the ties to prevent and/or extinguish fires in areas where heavy breaking was required. Tie fires were usually caused by hot molten metal falling from the cast iron engine brake shoes. The sprayers were controlled by hand operated valves which are located above the sprayer header, below the tender frame. Compare these "tie" sprayers with "Driver Tire Cooling Water Spray Valve,"

Tool Boxes: There is a tool box on the front of the tender accessible from the monkey deck and one below the tender on the right side between the trucks. The one between the tender trucks usually contained a re-railing frog for re-railing wheels, and spare coupler knuckles. It also contained several oak blocks used to place under the frog when it was being used.

Weight: The weight of the tender loaded with water and oil was 393,300 lb.

Wheel Cooling Water Sprayers: The tender is equipped with sprayers over each wheel that were used in conjunction with the sprayers over the locomotive drive wheel tires (see "Driver Tire Cooling Water Spray Valve," p.33). The tender wheel sprayers are difficult to see; use a flash light and look under the tender to see them.

12: Valve Gear

A – Boiler stay bolts
B – Air filter
C – Curved link
D – Yoke
E – Mechanical lubricator pump
F – Steam line to passenger cars
G – Adjustment ports for valve cylinders
H – Brake shoe
I – Drive wheel with counter balance weight
J – Main rod
K – Drive rod
L – Cross head
M – Valve cylinder
N – Main cylinder

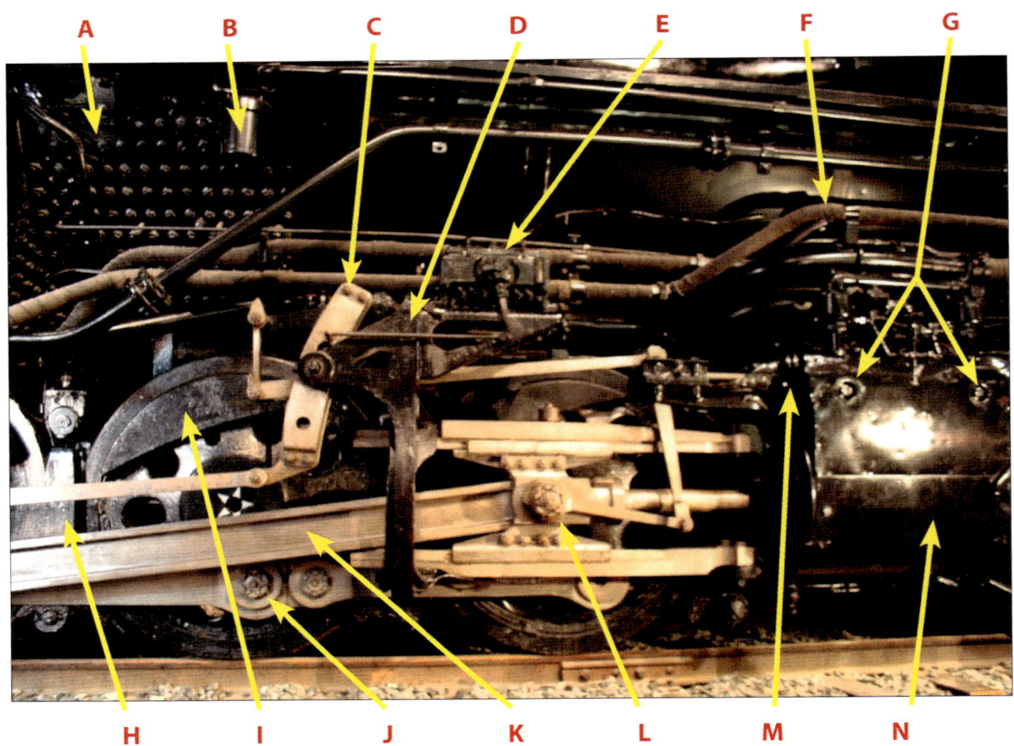

Figure 39 – Walschaert Valve Gear

Walschaert Valve Gear: The valve gear consists of a lever (see "Power Reversing Lever," p.39) located to the left of the engineer's seat, with linkage to an ALCO Type H pneumatic power reverser on the right side of the locomotive. The linkage from this booster is connected to the four link-blocks that are inserted in four curved links located just forward of each set of cylinders (see Figure 39 above).

The blocks are connected to the piston rods of the steam valve cylinders located just above the main cylinders. The curved links are connected to the return crank on the second set of drive wheels on each set of drivers. The links are mounted on a pivot and are rocked back and forth by this crank. During operation the rocking of the curved links causes the piston in the valve cylinders to move back and forth. A movement of the reversing lever by the engineer when running could change the status of the link blocks in the curved links. This action could shorten or lengthen the stroke of the valve piston. Changing the stroke of the valve piston would adjust the amount of steam entering the main pistons. By manipulating the amount of steam available, the engineer could increase or decrease the power and efficiency of the locomotive. Once the locomotive was moving and had gained some momentum, a lesser amount of steam was needed to maintain its operation. When stopped the full opposite execution of the power reversing lever would place the locomotive into the reverse mode.

Adjustment Ports: On each end of the steam valve cylinders are two 2-inch ports fitted with plugs (see Figure 39 above). The plugs were removed to perform tests on the integrity and location of the valve piston.

At 60 mph a drive wheel with a diameter of 5' 6" revolves five times per second. A main piston rod moves back and forth every time the driver wheel makes one revolution, thus it moves back or forth ten times per second. At speed, the precise setting of the stroke of the valve piston was one of the critical adjustments that had to be done properly.

Running Backwards: When the locomotives were, in effect, turned around to form the Cab-forwards they had to be redesigned. One of the problems that needed to be addressed was the position of the link blocks on the curved links. While running, the link blocks would be at the top of the curved links on the Walschaert valve gear because the engine would essentially be running at what was formerly backwards (see Figure 39 above). This position was not mechanically desirable so the drive wheel cranks were rotated 180 degrees, which lowered the link blocks to the bottom of the curved links where they were intended to be during normal (forward) operation. This position was desirable because if a reverse link broke, being at the bottom, the locomotive would keep moving forward.

Under Maximum Steam: When starting out or climbing a

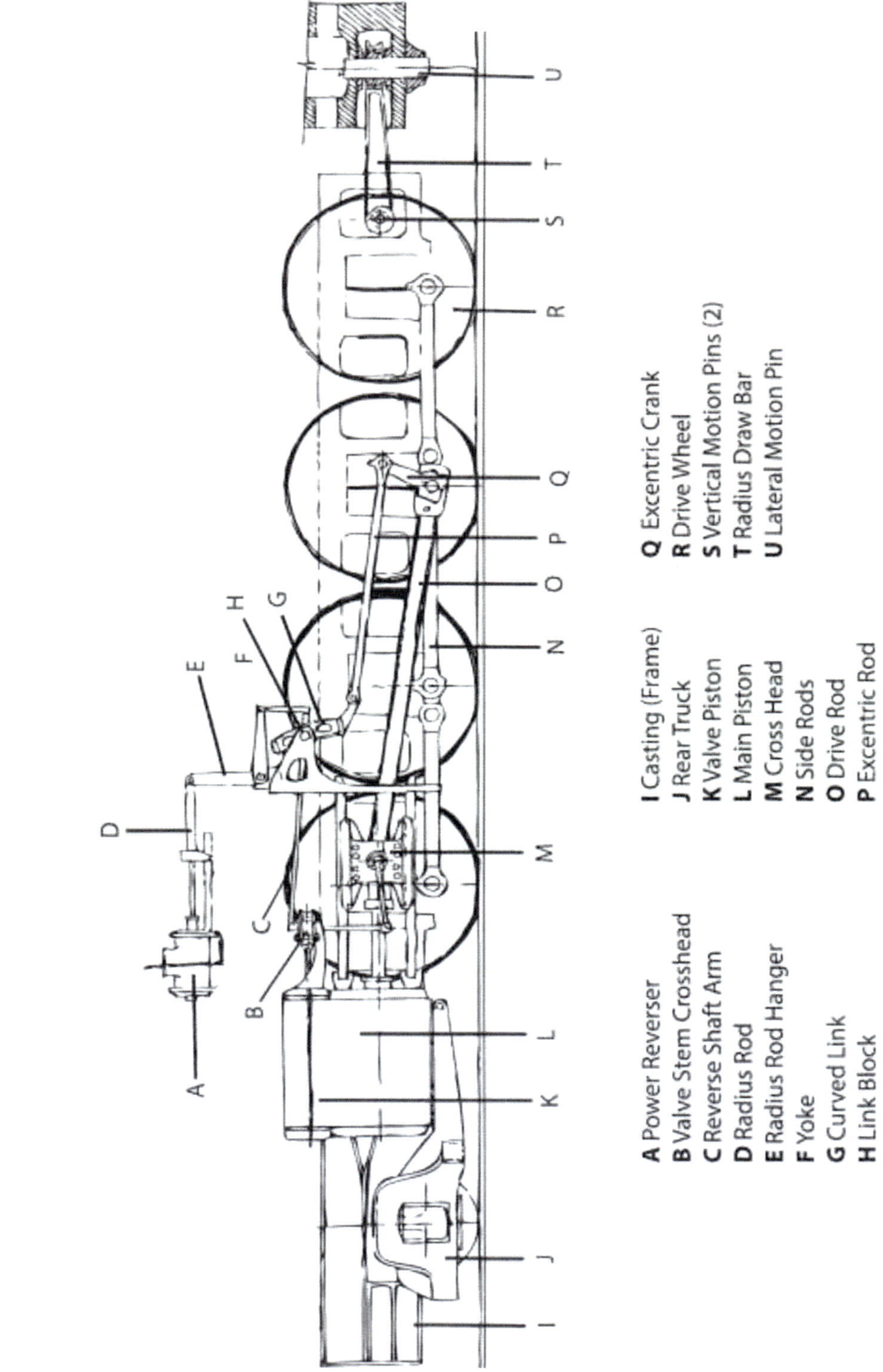

Figure 40 – Walschaert Valve Gear (Details)

heavy grade the link blocks would be at the bottom of the curved links. This was referred to by railroaders as being "down in the corner." Running down in the corner used a lot of steam. So as soon as some momentum was gained the engineer would notch (back off) the reversing lever to conserve steam.

13: Maintenance

Maintenance Levels: There were five maintenance levels corresponding to the passage of time and miles. They are as follows:

Trip Inspection and Minor Maintenance: After every trip an engine crew foreman or an inspector would compile a list of problems that had to be addressed. These items would be copied by a clerk onto cards and placed in a set of employee boxes depending on what needed to be fixed. For example, work orders that needed to be done by a machinist, pipe fitter, boiler maker, etc., were placed in the appropriate boxes for workers with the necessary skills. These were referred to as "Class Repairs" and numbered in order of one to five; see below for details. Sometimes not all of the repairs were completed before the locomotive was taken out on its next trip. However, at no time was a locomotive sent out on a run in an unsafe condition. All safety problems had to be addressed.

Quarterly Maintenance: A quarterly maintenance included the fixing of problems of a more serious nature like peeling tires, changing brake shoes and maintenance on appliances.

Semi Annual Maintenance: The semi-annual maintenance involved heavier duty tasks.

Annual Maintenance: An annual maintenance included some boiler work, replacing driver tires, appliance testing and repairs, work on articulation and tender couplings, brakes, drive rods, bearings, trucks and other major components.

Complete Rebuild: After several years of operation locomotives would be completely stripped and rebuilt. The usable life of a Cab-forward was about 25 to 30 years.

Super Heater Maintenance: Back shop employees did not like to work on Cab-forward super heaters. It required disconnecting the tender, which added more work to an already tedious, but critical job.

Reciprocating Equipment: The heavy weight of the reciprocating equipment required extensive and continued repairs. This was a common problem with all steam locomotives.

Personnel: It has been reported that twenty to twenty-four locomotive maintenance workers were employed for every Cab-forward in operation on the SP system.

Boiler Test: The boiler was tested to 25 psi above the operating pressure of 250 psi at least every 12 months. The three pop-off safety valves would be closed and the boiler pressure would be brought up to 275 psig for a pressure test.

Boiler Washout (cleaning): Periodically, locomotives would be shopped to clean the boiler. When the fire box was cold enough (about 75 degrees) all of the washout plugs would be removed and the annulus between the fire box combustion chamber and the boiler housing would be washed out with high pressure hoses. When the washing was complete all of the washout plugs were replaced except one that was close to the normal working water level. The boiler would be refilled up to the open washout plug and made ready to steam up again.

Inspectors

Federal Lead Inspectors: These inspectors were railroad employees who were sanctioned by the Federal Interstate Commerce Commission Inspectors. They did the day-to-day shop inspections and signed off on most of the completed work.

Federal Inspectors: They would arrive from time to time and check up on the Lead Inspectors. They had the final say on whether a repair or mechanical problem would or would not pass.

Southern Pacific Classification of Steam Locomotive Repairs

Class 5: Renewal of drivers, engine, and trailing trucks, renewal and turning of tires, necessary repairs to machinery and tender.

Class 4: Same as Class 5, except also partial set of flues.

Class 3: Same as Class 5, with full set of flues

Class 2: New firebox, or one or more shell courses, or roof sheet, flues new or reset, tires turned or new, general repairs to machinery and tender.

Class 1: Complete rebuild, new boiler or new back end, flues new or reset, tires turned or new, general repairs to machinery and tender.

14: Emplacement of the Locomotive in the Museum

One of the most frequently asked questions is how this engine was moved into the museum. Some visitors actually believe that the building was built around it, but that was not the case. It was done with two diesel locomotives and the turn table. Diesel number one was run from the turn table into the round house then through a switch and onto a track in the round house adjacent to the one to be used by the Cab-forward. The 4294 was pushed onto the turntable by diesel number two, and diesel number two was then uncoupled. While on the turn table the locomotive was so well balanced that the table was easily turned with its air motor. There was about six inches of clearance on each end. The 4294 was aligned to the proper track by the turn table. A cable was attached from the diesel number one to the Cab-forward and it was slowly pulled off the turn table and into the round house. Diesel locomotive number two was then run onto the turn table and aligned with the Cab-forward in the round house. It then gently pushed the Cab-forward to its present position. Note the tender was brought in prior to the Cab-forward in the same manner but, it was so light that it did not present any difficulties.

The rail on which the Cab-forward rests is 132 Ib. Also note that the rail from the turn table to just forward of the locomotive is probably in the 90 to 100 Ib. range. When the track upon which the locomotive sits was installed it was not aligned properly to the track from the turn table pit. Thus there was a slight crook at the joint. This mistake caused the installation crew to adjust the lighter track to fit the heaver track. The obvious distortion in the lighter rail where it meets the heaver rail is the result of this work.

The engine rests on a 132-pound rail which, in turn, rests on standard tie plates, cross ties, and rock ballast. Beneath the ballast is a reinforced concrete slab about two feet thick. Beneath the slab are two rows of 12-inch by 12-inch pre-stressed concrete pilings that were driven about 70 feet into the earth fill and river silt below. Each pile was designed to carry a 70 ton load, which, when combined, is double the calculated load of the locomotive. This measure was necessary to support the enormous weight of this machine.

As an aside, 45-ton-rated piles were driven under the rest of the museum except under the bridge carrying the narrow gauge train. Here 70-ton-rated piles were driven. Also 40-ton-rated piles were driven below the rolling stock storage tracks inside the replica of the 1867 passenger station, which is located a short distance south of the museum.

While driving the piles during the construction of the museum, what was believed to be a circa middle 1800s lock shop was found where the north east corner of the museum now stands. The floor of this shop was about 20 feet below the present floor level. Several Chinese pottery artifacts were also found in or near this site, all of which were broken, indicating that it was possibly near a dump site on the south shore of what was then called Sutter Lake and later China Lake. This is consistent with early historical reports that the north side of I street was inhabited by Chinese.

Above: Publicity photo of cab forward SP #4162 and C.P. Huntington, SP #1, taken in Sacramento in 1937 to emphasize the change in size and power of Southern Pacific's steam locomotives. The Huntington was built in 1863 as the third locomotive for the Central Pacific. After formation of the second Southern Pacific, in 1870, it became S.P. #1. Scott Inman collection

15: Cab-Forward Selected Mishaps

The early Cab-forwards had only a single-axle front truck. In 1912 Cab-forward MC-4 No. 4208 (a 2-6-6-2 built in 1911) derailed west bound near Applegate on the line over the Sierra. It was determined that the single-axle front truck was the probable cause. To solve that problem, two-axle front trucks were installed on all new Cab-forwards starting in 1913. The 4208 derailed on its maiden run westbound.

In 1914 an AC-3, built in 1913, blew up at Dutch Flat on the Roseville Subdivision of the Donner Pass route due to low water level. The blast caused the death of the crew. This unit was less than two years old, but was rebuilt in the Sacramento shops in 1914.

In the spring of 1930 AC-2 4017 (built in 1929) blew up between Weed California and Ashland, Oregon (Shasta Division). An ICC investigation concluded that low water level in the boiler exposed the crown sheet causing the explosion. The engineer was killed, but the fireman survived because he was out on the cat walk trying to get the boiler check valve working. He was blown clear of the locomotive. Because this route has exceptionally steep grades (3%), which causes boiler water to surge downhill depending on whether the locomotive is ascending or descending, the ICC prohibited the use of articulated locomotives on this portion of the Shasta Division. In this case the locomotive was running uphill causing the boiler water to shift toward the smoke box end, exposing the crown sheet.

In 1941 the boiler of AC-8 No. 4199 blew up near Cooper in the Salinas Valley (about 4 miles north of Salinas). The blast killed the crew of four and hurled the boiler 107 feet away. The fire box casing sheets and sides were blown 491 feet from the locomotive frame. Other parts were hurled as far as 562 feet away. The four persons who were killed were riding in the cab. It was reported that a fifth person died, but he was not on the train

In 1941 SP 4193 burned up in the Santa Susana Pass Tunnel just northwest of Chatsworth in Southern California. As the slow moving 96-car train ascended the grade built into the 7,359 foot long tunnel it stalled. It then slipped backwards, and during an attempt to get the engine pulling again a knuckle broke, separating the train line and causing an emergency brake application. The tunnel then filled with smoke, and the engine caught fire, killing four crew members. The fire also caused the death of a rear end brakeman.

In 1954 Cab-forward AC-10 No. 4231 was east bound on the point of an extra on SP's Western Division (Oakland to Roseville). The 4231 was following a train that had passed them minutes before at Fairfield-Suisun. It was before dawn, winter time and a dense fog in the delta and the central valley had reduced the visibility to a few feet. The 4231 soon encountered a yellow block signal and as per the rules reduced speed and expected to find the next signal red. This was not the case, it was green. So the engineer resumed track speed of 55 mph. As they proceeded they encountered a series of yellow then green signals and the engineer mistakenly thought this would be the case for the entire run. However, the preceding train had stopped at the Davis yard to set out a car with a hot journal box leaving the caboose out on the main in the fog. Because the caboose was within the yard limits no flag was necessary. However the rear end brakeman of this train, being aware of the following train, put out a fusee, but not in time to stop the oncoming 4231. The engineer of the 4231 put the train into emergency, but it was too late; the 4231 plowed into the caboose. The porch on the caboose over-rode the pilot beam on the engine, forcing the main air reservoir tanks up under the cab floor and rupturing steam lines to various appliances. The engineer and fireman were able to jump clear but the front end brakeman was trapped and scalded. Both the engineer and fireman survived but the brakeman died shortly afterward.

16: General Comments

AC-6s: AC-6s were the first to have Worthington Type 6 feed water heaters.

AC-9s: AC-9s were conventional coal burning 2-8-8-4 (Yellowstone) locomotives. They were used in the southwest and later converted to oil to be used between Sparks, Nevada and Alturas, California and Fernley, Nevada. They could not be used in the Sierra snow sheds because of the excessive overhang on their pilots and the fact that they were conventional front stack units not Cab-forwards. Built by Lima, they were built to haul freight between El Paso, TX, and Tucumcari, NM. Yellowstone locomotives were much hotter to operate than a Cab-forward because there was very little ventilation.

AC-12s: Twenty AC-12s were ordered in 1943, and the last one built was the 4294. It was delivered in March of 1944.

Adhesion: The capacity of a locomotive to draw loads is dependent on the adhesion (also called "tractive effort") from the weight of the drive wheels on the rails. In ordinary weather adhesion it is equal to about one fifth of the weight of the drivers on the rails. When it is perfectly dry and the rails are clean it is about one fourth. When the rails are sanded it is about one third.

Boiler Capacity: As far as a locomotive is concerned, fast time, especially with heavy trains, is generally dependent more on the supply of steam than the size of the wheels. Speed, therefore, is to a great extent a question of boiler capacity and the general condition of the locomotive. A boiler must be within the limits of the locomotive's weight and space; it cannot be made too large.

Boiler Explosions: The amount of water in the boiler was a critical factor. If the water level dropped below the crown sheet (the top of the fire box) for a period of time the metal would weaken and the boiler could explode with devastating force. The explosion could hurl the boiler several hundred feet. Because of this aspect the crews on steam engines were constantly vigilant on the amount of water in the boiler.

Cab Heat: The temperature in the cab was about 10 to 15 degrees hotter than the outside temperature when the locomotive was in motion. When the locomotive was at rest on a hot day in the Central Valley of California the heat must have been almost unbearable.

Concurrent Operation: During the heyday of the Cab-forward locomotives, SP had an average of 105 in service at any given time.

Cost: In 1944 the cost of constructing an AC-12 was $251,000, and they could be built in a few months. The appliances were built by contractors and were off-the-shelf items.

Donner Pass Water Stops: AC locomotives used an excessive amount of water. On a heavy train over the Sierra a Cab-forward tender would have to be filled at least two times and possibly three if there was a delay. Because of the number of engines on a train a procedure was developed to water the locomotives in the shortest time possible. The Cab-forward and the helper engine would stop at optimally spaced water plugs and take on water. The Cab-forward ahead of the caboose and several cars would cut off and back down to another water plug. Then the Cab-forward and the cars ahead of the caboose would cut loose and back down to a water plug between the train and the water plug servicing the last locomotive. It took about 15 minutes to fill a 22,000 gallon Cab-forward tender. Water plugs on the west slope were located at Colfax, Gold Run, Emigrant Gap, and Norden.

Driver Diameter: The diameter of the drivers was increased from 57 inches to 63 inches on AC-4s in 1928. This allowed the engines to travel at a higher rate of speed, which also made them useful for passenger engines.

Dry Steam Source: Most locomotives use dry steam to operate various appliances like air pumps, feed pumps and blowers. When a locomotive is just standing the super heater tubes are still filled with dry steam. A side connection built into the super heater system allowed steam to be drawn off through a nipple on the left side of the smoke box. This steam access point on the 4294 supplied dry steam to the whistle, air compressors, feed pump, and to the super-heated steam header in the cab.

Drive Wheel Dynamics and Piston Valves: At 60 mph a drive wheel with a diameter of 63 inches revolves about 5.3 times every second (see calculations below). A 32-inch long piston rod moves back and forth every time the driver makes one revolution, or ten times a second. At this rate of speed the setting of the stroke of a valve piston is critical.

Calculation of driver revolutions per second

63 inch drive wheel X 3.14 = a circumference of 197.8 inches
5,280 feet in a mile X 12 inches = 63,360 inches per mile
63,360 inches / 197.8 inches = 320.3 revolutions per mile
320.3 / 60 seconds in a minute = 5.3 revolutions per second

Exhaust Coloration: The fireman could maintain a proper fire by observing the color of the exhaust smoke. If the smoke was light gray (i.e., he could see through it), he had a proper fire. If the smoke was black, too much oil was being fed into the fire box. **Freight Train Capability:** In the flat land of the Great Valley of California an AC was expected to handle 80 to 100 freight cars. An AC could pull 40 to 50 loaded freight cars over Donner Summit.

Fruit Block Trains: Most fruit block trains consisted of all refrigerator cars from approximately 80 to 120 cars. A Cab-forward and another helper engine were usually on the point, a Cab-forward may be placed about the center of the train and a third was cut in a few cars ahead of the caboose.

Getting Underway: The full horsepower of a steam locomotive at rest is almost nil because motion is required before the locomotive can start to produce work. Once a steam engine is underway the horsepower potential begins to kick in. However, a steam engine at rest can develop full torque at zero rpm. Therefore, to start a heavy train from scratch using a steam engine was extremely difficult and sometimes nearly impossible. The technique employed was to put the engine into reverse for a few feet to bunch up the couplers on the train, then turn on the sanders and start moving forward. As the engine began to move forward it would only be starting one car at a time, then another, and another. Once some momentum was achieved the remaining cars would be pulled into motion. Sometimes the engineer would have to employ this technique two or three times to get underway. The engineer had to be careful not to increase the speed before the entire train was in motion or a coupler knuckle or draw bar could be broken. This starting problem was directly related to the fact that at that time almost all rolling stock had friction bearings.

Harmonic Motion: At about 45 mph, a Cab-forward, if not under a load, would enter a period of harmonic motion. This motion could amount to several hundred pounds of pressure on the drivers. During this motion the locomotive's drivers would actually be bouncing off the rails. The floor in the cab would bounce about 3 to 4 inches, and it was hard to keep one's feet on the floor. It was also hard to walk about without bending your knees. Somewhere around 47 or 48 mph the locomotive would stabilize and run smoother, similar to passing through a sound barrier.

Horsepower: The horsepower of a locomotive is calculated at full throttle. The formula to calculate horsepower is PLAN/33,000 where "P" is the effective pressure in the cylinders during running (usually taken as half the boiler pressure), "L" is the piston stroke in feet, "A" is the area of the drive cylinder, in square inches, and "N" is the locomotive's speed in strokes per minute, counting strokes on both sides of the piston. At a working speed of 45 to 50 mph this locomotive developed approximately 6,000 horsepower.

Minimum Curve: The minimum curve that a Cab-forward could negotiate was 18 degrees.

Passenger Train Capability: An AC could handle 12 to 14 heavy weight passenger cars over the Sierra.

Noise: The noise level in the cab was considerable. While running, crew members had to shout to one another to be heard. The greatest source of noise in the cab was the fire box. Noise was also created by the release of compressed air during braking. This is true of any steam locomotive.

Oil Temperature: It was important to keep the injection temperature of the fuel oil into the fire box above 160 to 170 degrees (F). If the oil was too cold the spray or atomizer nozzle could not handle it. This condition would cause excess oil to run on the ground below the locomotive.

Reliability: The later Cab-forwards were extremely reliable engines. They had economic problems in common with all other steam locomotives, but they could pull a train over a distance of 500 miles without having to service the engine. Typically Cab-forwards would travel over several thousand miles a month.

Repairs: It has been said that for every Cab-forward in service the Southern Pacific Railroad had 20 to 24 shop personnel on the payroll. There is no better example of the difficulties in maintaining these locomotives than the changing of a boiler tube. First the tender had to be disconnected and the feed water heater had to be pulled from the smoke box, usually with some difficulty. This was followed by the removal of the super heater tubes. With this accomplished they could address the replacement of the faulty tube. When one considers the size of these locomotives it is easy to imagine the work that had to be done in the repair or replacement of any boiler or running gear hardware.

Reversing Lever: The use of the reversing lever was critical during the normal operation of these locomotives. Starting out with a heavy train, the lever would be at the forward end of the toothed radius. This was called "down in the corner," or maximum steam pressure to the pistons. On the sides of a locomotive with Walschaert running gear the reversing shaft arm would be at the bottom of the curved links. This is what "down in the corner" looked like. As the locomotive began to gain speed the engineer would begin to move the lever toward the center of the radius. This action was necessary and important because it conserved steam. While running on the road, the engineer would change the position of the reversing lever to meet the various grades encountered. This was called "hooking up or down" depending on the percentage of the grade to be overcome. The movement of the lever would actually shorten or lengthen the stroke of the valve piston. Each significant movement of the lever required action by the fireman to match the steam being used.

Saturated Steam: Saturated steam was needed for the Injectors and hydrostatic oilers. Wet steam would condense readily and produce the mass of the condensate that created the overpressure needed to force the water and lubricant into the boiler and steam pipes. Most of the copper tubing that was connected to gauges and controls in the cab, as well as those on the Nathan lubricating pumps, is missing from 4294.

Saturation Temperature: At 250 psi pressure in the boiler, water boils at about 400.9 degrees F. This is called the "saturation temperature" of the steam in the boiler. The throttle valve in the 4294 is located on the downstream side of the super heater. The pressure in the super heater is the same pressure as that in the boiler. When the throttle is opened, 400.9 degree (F) steam passes through the many small super heater tubes which are inserted into the larger boiler tubes. The pressure remains the same but the temperature of the steam now rises to around 650 to 700 degrees F or higher. As the steam enters the pistons with its highly elevated temperature it now has a tremendous ability to do a significant amount of work. The pressure drops to about 225 psi due to flow restrictions as it enters the pistons. The superheated steam will decline in temperature but not to the point where it will condense on the walls of the cylinder and main pistons. It is important not to have condensate form in the cylinders as it could lower their efficiency. When in full operation some superheated steam will be exhausting out of the locomotive smoke stacks along with the gasses from the fire box. The condensate would shower down on the Monkey Deck.

SP Cab-forward Donation: In late 1957 or early 1958 Southern Pacific offered three Cab-forwards to anyone willing to take them. The City of Sacramento was the only taker. The 4294 was placed in a park in front of the Sacramento Railroad Station on October 20, 1958. It was removed in 1967. Unfortunately, the locomotive was stripped of most of its copper metal parts by vandals during the nine or so years it sat there. A few of these parts, in particular gauges, have been replaced.

Tonnage Capacity: SP rated the 4294's towing capacity at 7,000 to 9,000 tons.

Tractive Effort: The best way to evaluate the ability of a steam engine was to measure its tractive effort. This is essentially the weight a locomotive can pull before its driving wheels begin to slip. The tractive effort for the 4294 was rated at 124,300 pounds at the draw bar. It is essentially the weight a locomotive can pull before its drivers begin to slip.

Turn Tables: There were three turn tables that could handle Cab-forwards over Donner Pass: Roseville and Norden, California, and Sparks, Nevada. There was also a balloon track at Truckee that was used to turn locomotives including cab-forwards.

Water Use: While pulling heavy grades sometimes both the injector and the feed water pump were used to supply water to the boiler. Also on heavy grades 11,000 gallons of water an hour could be used. This was the equivalent of half the water in the tender. On a normal trip over the Sierra the Cab-forward tenders would have to be filled two or three times.

Above: SP #4000 at Reno, Nevada, in May 1909. Stanley Palmer photo

17: Selected References

The Association of American Railroads – ***Locomotive Cyclopedias*** 1938, 1941, 1942 and 1944, CSRM Library

Carroll, Terry – ***What's That Thing For?*** CSRM docent handouts, no date

Church, Robert, J. – ***Cab-forward – The Story of Southern Pacific Articulated Locomotives,*** 1982, Central Valley Railroad Publications, Wilton, CA

Fidler, Lane – ***Steam Locomotive Training Manual***, California State Railroad Museum, 1981

Harlan, George H. – ***Those Amazing Cab-forwards,*** 1983, Published by George H. Harlan, Greenbrae, CA

Harding, J.W. – ***Walschaert Valve Gear***, 1943, International Textbook Co.

Lawmaster, Oliver – ***Operating The Cab-forward***, CSRM docent publication, 2001

Masklee, Chris – ***Railroad History Building Off To Solid Start***, 1978, Sample 28, Random Samples, Caltrans

Signor, John R. – ***Donner Pass – Southern Pacific's Sierra Crossing***, 1985, Golden West Books, San Marino CA

Smith, Harry – ***DVD No. D2045***, CSRM Docent Library, 1998

(Unknown) – Locomotive Record (card) for the Southern Pacific 4294, March 5, 1956, on file at the CSRM

Westinghouse Air Brake Co. – ***No. 8-ET Locomotive Brake Equipment, No. 5032-1,*** 1937, Pittsburgh, PA

Worthington Pump and Machinery Corp. – ***Locomotive Feed Water Heater Type S***, 1929, Harrison NJ

Worthington Pump and Machinery Corp. – ***Locomotive Feed Water Heating Equipment, No. W-220-ELE***, 1947, Harrison NJ

Above: Cab-forward AC-7 #4170 at Nevada Dock near Martinez, California, in 1954. Fred Matthews Photo, Scott Inman Collection

18: Personal Communications

The authors would like to thank the following individuals for their personal involvement and generous technical contributions in the development of this work. Without them, the document could not have been completed with a high level of accuracy.

Carroll, Terry: Mr. Carroll provided an invaluable critique of a draft of this document and references to important publications in the CSRM library containing details on many aspects of the 4294.

Church, Robert: Dr. Church, an author of a well-known publication on ACs, resolved many of the questions that plagued the authors during the early preparation of this document. His encouragement to bring it to completion helped to make it happen.

Prizmitch, Tony: Mr. Prizmitch is a retired SP machinist and a steam locomotive inspector with a background of working with ACs. The authors thank him for the time and effort he expended showing us the details and intricacies of this machine on his three different visits to the CSRM.

Ryden, Karl: Mr. Ryden is a long-time Southern Pacific employe who worked out of Roseville, California as an engineer on Cab-forwards over Donner Pass. His input was invaluable concerning the air brake systems, operating procedures, and general background information.

Tinkham, Calvin: Mr. Tinkham, a retired SP fireman who worked ACs out of Sparks, Nevada, was invaluable in his technical review of the paper and on a hands-on visit to the CSRM to detail the many features of the 4294. He builds 7.5-inch gauge live steam locomotives.

Wyatt, Kyle: Mr. Wyatt, the Curator of History and Technology at the CSRM, provided invaluable help in the preparation of this document through advice on document research in the Museum library, consultation toward the solution of various problems, insights on where information could be found, and a photograph of the inside of the turret of the 4294.

Yee, Wesley: Mr. Yee was the civil engineering inspector on the site preparation for the CSRM in the late 1970s. His description of the pilings driven under the Museum building and the passenger station provided an insight into the planning and preparation needed to display this locomotive.

Above: Close-up of the tender of AC-12 #4288 in the 1950s. Art Laidlaw Photo, Chris Stark Collection

19: About the Authors

David N. Anderson

David N. Anderson was born in 1932 in Glendale and raised in Canoga Park. In the 1950s he spent a two-year hitch in the U.S. Army. After discharge from the Army, Dave attended UCLA where he received a degree in geology in 1962. He worked as a geologist for the State of California for several years and eventually became involved in geothermal energy. In 1976 he became the Executive Director of the Geothermal Resources Council, a nonprofit membership association located in Davis, California. In 1997, Dave organized and became the Executive Director of the AEEES, a nonprofit association focusing on ground source heat pumps.

Dave became a docent at the California State Railroad Museum in Sacramento in 1998. He has logged more than 5,000 volunteer hours including as a narrator providing historical information on Amtrak trains traveling between Sacramento and Reno. Growing up in Southern California, he witnessed the operation of cab-forward locomotives, which peaked his interest in the museum's cab-forward. He lives with his wife Eva in Davis California. They have been married for more than 60 years.

Vincent C. Cipolla

Left: Vince Cipolla in his final year as a Southern Pacific Employe at San Luis Obispo, California. Mark Hornbeck Photo

Few men employed by the Southern Pacific Railroad have laid claim to firing and operating steam power over their division which weighed in excess of one million pounds. One such individual who has experienced the thrill of commanding a mighty cab forward over the Tehachapi Mountains of California has also dedicated his life to the preservation of the beloved "Malleys," as crews so fondly remember them. Also widely known in the Southern Pacific community as "The Godfather," retired San Joaquin Division Locomotive Engineer Vincent C. Cipolla retired in 1989 with the highest seniority of anyone in his same craft on his division.

The Godfather hired out with the Southern Pacific during the depths of World War II on May 9, 1943 and served his first assignment as a store keeper at the oil house located within SP's Los Angeles General Shops. He worked distributing heavy grease lubricant known as "pin dope" to the roundhouse and servicing facilities on the Los Angeles Division. In February 1944 Cipolla was transferred to the Mission Road Coach Yard where he worked as an electrician's assistant on baggage and RPO equipment. He was frequently sent from the coach yard to the relatively new Los Angeles Union Passenger Terminal to service lamps and electric lights on passenger cars.

During the remainder of the war and until December 1945, Vince bid a job working at the Taylor Roundhouse in Los Angeles. There he was an apprentice electrician and performed minor wiring repairs, bulb replacements, and servicing inspections of motive power. However, Cipolla's next assignment would begin his legacy of more than 40 continuous years of engine service as a member of Southern Pacific's Operating Department—a career that would earn him the title of "The Godfather."

Following several weeks of unpaid training runs, Vince Cipolla would officially become a certified locomotive fireman on January 2, 1946 on the San Joaquin Division operating between Los Angeles and Bakersfield California. This section of the Southern Pacific was dominated by large locomotives, and cab forwards ruled on the San Joaquin. His experience as a fireman would lend opportunities in both freight and passenger service, and Vince quickly learned to shadow the best and most knowledgeable engineers that operated cab forwards. In effort to advance his understanding of proper handling on the AC class engines, he would politely interview and question the engineers on their techniques. On one occasion when a cab forward began "riding rough" and experienced harmonics, Cipolla turned to a more senior engineer who was a boomer from the Denver & Rio Grande Western Railroad. The engineer quickly showed Vince exactly how to adjust both the throttle and reverser so the engine would settle into rhythm against the opposing forces of driving rods and counterbalances on each engine.

June of 1951 was the month that fulfilled Cipolla's dream of becoming a qualified engineer for the Southern Pacific. He would remain an engineer in train service until September of 1989 when he retired. After operating his last 4-8-8-2 in 1956, The Godfather never forgot his experiences on steam, and has made an effort to preserve his operational knowledge of these machines through numerous contributions. These include editing of publications for historical accuracy, organizing oral history panels for the Southern Pacific Historical & Technical Society, and through a starring role in an interpretive DVD titled *Southern Pacific 4294, The Last Cab Forward.*

When asked about his final reflections on the 4294, The Godfather was quoted as noting "I never had such a finer pleasure in my life than to be a part of these machines, and to the men of the San Joaquin Division and the Grand Ole Southern Pacific, I thank you for the opportunity. One more time; thank you."

He is one of the last of the last, if not the last, who can say, "I was an engineer on a Cab-forward."

Russell M.H. O'Day

Russell M.H. O'Day (Russ) was born in 1919 and grew up in Colorado. He enlisted in the Army in 1937 and served in the Army and Air Force for nearly 32 years, retiring as a Lt. Colonel in 1969. During WW2 he flew B-24s and other aircraft in the Pacific. After retiring from the military he worked in the communications industry and later founded a commercial travel agency in Sacramento. He passed in 2018.

Russ was a graduate of Sacramento State University and served as a docent at the CSRM starting in 1998. He logged more than 5,000 hours of volunteer time, including as a narrator on Amtrak trains between Sacramento and Reno, and specialized in Cab-forward 4294.

Appendix: AC-Class Summary and Roster Details

AC-Class SP Cab Forward Summary

Class	Cab #s	# in Class	Whyte	Boiler Pres, PSI	Tractive Effort, Pounds	Comments
AC-1	4000–4016	17	2-8-8-2	210	90,940	Rebuilt from MC-1
AC-2	4017–4028	12	2-8-8-2	210	90,940	Rebuilt from MC-4
AC-3	4029–4048	20	2-8-8-2	210	90,940	Rebuilt from MC-6
AC-4	4100–4109	10	4-8-8-2	235	116,900	Built 1928, first 'modern' cab forwards
AC-5	4110–4125	16	4-8-8-2	235	116,900	Built 1929
AC-6	4126–4150	25	4-8-8-2	250	124,300	Built 1930, updated specs followed by all later
AC-7	4151–4176	26	4-8-8-2	250	124,300	Built 1937, introduced new cab & tender
AC-8	4177–4204	28	4-8-8-2	250	124,300	Built 1939
AC-9*	3800–3811	12	2-8-8-4	250	124,300	Built 1939, included for completeness
AC-10	4205–4244	40	4-8-8-2	250	124,300	Built 1942
AC-11	4245–4274	30	4-8-8-2	250	124,300	Built 1942
AC-12	4275–4294	20	4-8-8-2	250	124,300	Built 1944, last SP new steam locomotives.

* **Note:** Class AC-9 were conventional articulated locomotives that were technically similar to the AC-7 through AC-12. Originally coal-powered because SP had a contract to buy coal, they were designed to run between El Paso & Tucumcari, NM, where the cab forward configuration was unnecessary. They were converted to oil when the coal contract expired.

SP Cab Forward Roster Details						
Cab No.	Class	Whyte	Date In Service	Off Roster Date	Roster Years	Comments
3900	AM-2	4-6-6-2	9/19/11	5/22/47	35.7	Built as MM-2 #4200 (2-6-6-2); to 4-6-6-2 by 1914; simpled, 1928; r/n AM-2 #3900, 1938; SP scrapped 6/14/1947 at Sacramento. Among first 20 retired.
3901	AM-2	4-6-6-2	9/21/11	10/31/47	36.1	Built as MM-2 #4201 (2-6-6-2); to 4-6-6-2 by 1914; simpled, 1936; r/n AM-2 #3901, 1938; SP scrapped 11/10/1947.
3902	AM-2	4-6-6-2	10/17/11	8/21/48	36.8	Built as MM-2 #4202 (2-6-6-2); to 4-6-6-2, 1913; simpled, 1936; r/n AM-2 #3902, 1938; SP scrapped 8/21/1948. Top 20 service life.
3903	AM-2	4-6-6-2	10/14/11	10/21/46	35.0	Built as MM-2 #4203 (2-6-6-2); to 4-6-6-2 by 1914; simpled, 1936; r/n AM-2 #3903, 1938; SP scrapped 11/23/1946 at Sacramento. Shortest-service AM-2 Among first 20 retired.
3904	AM-2	4-6-6-2	10/18/11	4/12/47	35.5	Built as MM-2 #4204 (2-6-6-2); to 4-6-6-2 by 1914; simpled, 1936; r/n AM-2 #3904, 1938; SP scrapped 4/12/1947 at Sacramento. Among first 20 retired.
3905	AM-2	4-6-6-2	10/24/11	4/23/47	35.5	Built as MM-2 #4205 (2-6-6-2); to 4-6-6-2, 1914; simpled, 1929; r/n AM-2 #3905, 1938; among first 30 retired; SP scrapped 4/23/1947 at Sacramento.
3906	AM-2	4-6-6-2	11/4/11	12/24/47	36.1	Built as MM-2 #4206 (2-6-6-2); to 4-6-6-2, 1913; simpled, 1936; r/n AM-2 #3906, 1938; SP scrapped 12/24/1947
3907	AM-2	4-6-6-2	11/1/11	9/23/48	36.9	Built as MM-2 #4207 (2-6-6-2); to 4-6-6-2, 1913; simpled, 1937; r/n AM-2 3907, 1938; SP scrapped 9/23/1948. Top 20 service life. Longest serving AM-2.
3908	AM-2	4-6-6-2	11/12/11	3/8/48	36.3	Built as MM-2 #4208 (2-6-6-2); to 4-6-6-2, 1913; simpled, 1936; r/n AM-2 #3908, 1938; SP scrapped 3/8/1948
3909	AM-2	4-6-6-2	11/18/11	1/12/48	36.2	Built as MM-2 #4209 (2-6-6-2); to 4-6-6-2, 1913; simpled, 1930; r/n AM-2 #3909, 1938; SP scrapped 1/12/1948
3910	AM-2	4-6-6-2	11/28/11	3/4/47	35.3	Built as MM-2 #4210 (2-6-6-2); to 4-6-6-2, 1913; simpled, 1937; r/n AM-2 #3910, 1938; SP scrapped 4/4/1947. Among first 20 retired.
3911	AM-2	4-6-6-2	12/4/11	6/30/47	35.6	Built as MM-2 #4211 (2-6-6-2); to 4-6-6-2, 1913; simpled, 1936; r/n AM-2 #3911, 1938; among first 30 retired; SP scrapped 4/4/1947. Among first 20 retired.
4000	AC-1	2-8-8-2	5/26/09	4/2/48	38.9	Built as conventional cab MC-1. SP rebuilt to cab forward 6/1923 (photos in Docent Lounge); simpled 1931; SP scrapped 4/2/1948. Top 20 service life.
4001	AC-1	2-8-8-2	5/30/09	5/23/47	38.0	Built as conventional cab MC-1. SP rebuilt to cab forward 4/1923; simpled 1931; one of first 30 retired; SP scrapped 6/14/1947 at Sacramento. Top 20 service life. Among first 20 retired.
4002	AC-1	2-8-8-2	2/4/10	8/16/47	37.5	First cab forward built, as MC-2; simpled, 1931; SP scrapped 8/16/1947 at Sacramento. Top 20 service life. Among first 20 retired.
4003	AC-1	2-8-8-2	2/12/10	3/17/48	38.1	Built as MC-2; simpled, 1928; SP scrapped 3/17/48 at Sacramento. Top 20 service life.
4004	AC-1	2-8-8-2	2/11/10	3/28/47	37.1	Built as MC-2; simpled, 1929; SP scrapped 3/28/47 at Sacramento. Top 20 service life. Among first 20 retired.

SP Cab Forward Roster Details						
Cab No.	Class	Whyte	Date In Service	Off Roster Date	Roster Years	Comments
4005	AC-1	2-8-8-2	2/12/10	10/29/47	37.7	Built as MC-2; simpled, 1929; SP scrapped 10/29/47 at Sacramento. Top 20 service life. Among first 20 retired.
4006	AC-1	2-8-8-2	2/17/10	8/30/47	37.5	Built as MC-2; simpled, 1929; SP scrapped 8/30/47 at Sacramento. Top 20 service life. Among first 20 retired.
4007	AC-1	2-8-8-2	2/12/10	10/21/46	36.7	Built as MC-2; simpled, 1929; SP scrapped 12/14/46 at Sacramento. Among first 20 retired.
4008	AC-1	2-8-8-2	2/19/10	2/26/48	38.0	Built as MC-2; simpled, 1930; SP scrapped 2/26/48 at Sacramento. Top 20 service life.
4009	AC-1	2-8-8-2	2/25/10	10/13/48	38.6	Built as MC-2; simpled, 1929; SP scrapped 11/3/48 at Sacramento. Top 20 service life.
4010	AC-1	2-8-8-2	3/3/10	12/31/47	37.8	Built as MC-2; simpled, 1928; SP scrapped 12/31/47 at Sacramento. Top 20 service life.
4011	AC-1	2-8-8-2	3/5/10	12/31/35	25.83	Built as MC-2; not simpled; SP scrapped 12/29/1936. One of first 3 retired.
4012	AC-1	2-8-8-2	3/4/10	8/23/48	38.5	Built as MC-2; simpled, 1929; SP scrapped 8/27/48 at Sacramento. Top 20 service life.
4013	AC-1	2-8-8-2	3/10/10	12/31/35	25.81	Built as MC-2; not simpled; SP scrapped 11/30/1936. Shortest-service AC-1. One of first 3 retired.
4014	AC-1	2-8-8-2	3/8/10	3/11/49	39.0	Built as MC-2; simpled, 1929; SP scrapped 4/12/49 at Sacramento. Longest-service AC-1. Longest service overall.
4015	AC-1	2-8-8-2	3/12/10	11/17/48	38.7	Built as MC-2; simpled, 1930; SP scrapped 12/28/48 at Sacramento. Top 20 service life.
4016	AC-1	2-8-8-2	3/14/10	7/8/48	38.3	Built as MC-2; simpled, 1930; SP scrapped 7/8/48 at Sacramento. Top 20 service life.
4017	AC-2	2-8-8-2	8/1/11	5/22/47	35.8	Built as MC-4; simpled, 1930; SP scrapped 6/14/47 at Sacramento. Among first 20 retired.
4018	AC-2	2-8-8-2	7/21/11	7/28/47	36.0	Built as MC-4; simpled, 1928; SP scrapped 6/30/47 at Sacramento. Among first 20 retired.
4019	AC-2	2-8-8-2	8/1/11	11/21/47	36.3	Built as MC-4; simpled, 1928; SP scrapped 11/21/1947
4020	AC-2	2-8-8-2	8/14/11	12/18/47	36.3	Built as MC-4; simpled, 1928; SP scrapped 12/18/1947
4021	AC-2	2-8-8-2	8/29/11	6/23/47	35.8	Built as MC-4; simpled, 1930; SP scrapped 6/30/1947 at Sacramento. Among first 20 retired.
4022	AC-2	2-8-8-2	8/26/11	12/31/35	24.4	Built as MC-4; not simpled; SP scrapped 11/30/1936 at Sacramento. Shortest-service AC-2. Shortest service overall.
4023	AC-2	2-8-8-2	9/8/11	2/28/47	35.5	Built as MC-4; simpled, 1930; SP scrapped 7/21/1947 at Sacramento. Among first 20 retired.
4024	AC-2	2-8-8-2	9/4/11	8/9/48	36.9	Built as MC-4; simpled, 1928; SP scrapped 2/5/1949 at Sacramento. Top 20 service life.
4025	AC-2	2-8-8-2	9/12/11	7/8/48	36.8	Built as MC-4; simpled, 1929; SP scrapped 7/8/1948 at Sacramento. Top 20 service life.
4026	AC-2	2-8-8-2	9/11/11	3/17/48	36.5	Built as MC-4; simpled, 1929; SP scrapped 3/17/1948 at Sacramento
4027	AC-2	2-8-8-2	9/16/11	12/17/48	37.3	Built as MC-4; simpled, 1930; SP scrapped 1/22/1949. Longest-service AC-2. Top 20 service life.

SP Cab Forward Roster Details						
Cab No.	**Class**	**Whyte**	**Date In Service**	**Off Roster Date**	**Roster Years**	**Comments**
4028	AC-2	2-8-8-2	10/4/11	7/29/48	36.8	Built as MC-4; simpled, 1928; SP scrapped 7/29/1948 at Sacramento. Top 20 service life.
4029	AC-3	2-8-8-2	2/17/12	1/27/47	34.9	Built as MC-6; simpled, 1929; SP scrapped 4/4/1947 at Sacramento. Among first 20 retired.
4030	AC-3	2-8-8-2	12/19/12	8/23/48	35.7	Built as MC-6; simpled, 1930; SP scrapped 10/19/1948.
4031	AC-3	2-8-8-2	12/20/12	4/13/49	36.3	Built as MC-6; simpled, 1930; SP scrapped 5/16/1949 at Sacramento.
4032	AC-3	2-8-8-2	12/21/12	8/8/49	36.6	Built as MC-6; simpled, 1930; SP scrapped 10/27/1949. Longest-service AC-3.
4033	AC-3	2-8-8-2	12/17/12	7/29/48	35.6	Built as MC-6; simpled, 1930; SP scrapped 7/29/1948
4034	AC-3	2-8-8-2	12/20/12	11/19/47	34.9	Built as MC-6; simpled, 1929; SP scrapped 11/19/1947
4035	AC-3	2-8-8-2	12/22/12	12/31/48	36.0	Built as MC-6; simpled, 1930; SP scrapped 2/5/1949
4036	AC-3	2-8-8-2	12/22/12	3/20/48	35.2	Built as MC-6; simpled, 1929; SP scrapped 3/20/1948
4037	AC-3	2-8-8-2	12/21/12	6/20/49	36.5	Built as MC-6; boiler exploded, 1914; simpled, 1930; SP scrapped 6/23/1949 at Sacramento.
4038	AC-3	2-8-8-2	1/3/13	3/17/48	35.2	Built as MC-6; simpled, 1937; SP scrapped 3/17/1948 at Sacramento.
4039	AC-3	2-8-8-2	12/23/12	11/11/47	34.9	Built as MC-6; simpled, 1930; SP scrapped 11/11/1947 at Sacramento.
4040	AC-3	2-8-8-2	1/9/13	10/21/46	33.8	Built as MC-6; simpled, 1930; SP scrapped 12/21/1946 at Sacramento. One of first 20 retired.
4041	AC-3	2-8-8-2	1/21/13	1/3/49	36.0	Built as MC-6; simpled, 1927; SP scrapped 3/14/1949 at Sacramento.
4042	AC-3	2-8-8-2	1/12/13	3/1/49	36.1	Built as MC-6; simpled, 1930; SP scrapped 3/1/1949 at Sacramento.
4043	AC-3	2-8-8-2	1/24/13	6/15/49	36.4	Built as MC-6; simpled, 1930; SP scrapped 8/20/1949
4044	AC-3	2-8-8-2	6/14/13	2/4/48	34.6	Built as MC-6; simpled, 1929; SP scrapped 2/4/1948 at Sacramento.
4045	AC-3	2-8-8-2	6/17/13	10/21/46	33.3	Built as MC-6; simpled, 1928; Scrapped 12/31/1946 at Sacramento. Shortest-service AC-3. One of first 20 retired.
4046	AC-3	2-8-8-2	7/17/13	12/22/47	34.4	Built as MC-6; simpled, 1929; SP scrapped 12/22/1947 at Sacramento.
4047	AC-3	2-8-8-2	7/10/13	5/27/49	35.9	Built as MC-6; simpled, 1937; SP scrapped 6/30/1949 at Sacramento
4048	AC-3	2-8-8-2	7/17/13	10/13/48	35.2	Built as MC-6; simpled, 1937; SP scrapped 11/3/1948 at Sacramento
4100	AC-4	4-8-8-2	10/27/28	11/10/53	25.0	First 4-8-8-2 cab forward built simple articulated. Scrapped 12/17/1953 at Sacramento.
4101	AC-4	4-8-8-2	11/9/28	11/10/53	25.0	SP scrapped 12/17/1953 at Sacramento.
4102	AC-4	4-8-8-2	11/15/28	3/19/53	24.3	SP scrapped 4/21/1953 at Sacramento.
4103	AC-4	4-8-8-2	11/16/28	3/19/53	24.3	SP scrapped 12/17/1953 at Sacramento.
4104	AC-4	4-8-8-2	12/7/28	11/24/54	26.0	To scrapper 1/3/1955.
4105	AC-4	4-8-8-2	12/8/28	1/22/53	24.1	SP scrapped 3/9/1953 at Sacramento.
4106	AC-4	4-8-8-2	12/13/28	1/22/53	24.1	SP scrapped 2/5/1953 at Sacramento. Shortest-service AC-4.

SP Cab Forward Roster Details						
Cab No.	**Class**	**Whyte**	**Date In Service**	**Off Roster Date**	**Roster Years**	**Comments**
4107	AC-4	4-8-8-2	12/22/28	5/25/55	26.4	To scrapper 6/27/1955.
4108	AC-4	4-8-8-2	12/21/28	5/25/55	26.4	To scrapper 6/28/1955. Longest-service AC-4.
4109	AC-4	4-8-8-2	1/5/29	11/24/54	25.9	To scrapper 1/3/1955.
4110	AC-5	4-8-8-2	8/16/29	12/12/52	23.3	SP scrapped 2/3/1953 at Sacramento. Shortest-service AC-5.
4111	AC-5	4-8-8-2	8/29/29	4/20/54	24.6	SP scrapped 5/20/1954 at Sacramento.
4112	AC-5	4-8-8-2	8/22/29	11/10/53	24.2	SP scrapped 11/25/1953 at Sacramento.
4113	AC-5	4-8-8-2	8/17/29	4/5/55	25.6	To scrapper 5/6/1955. Longest-service AC-5.
4114	AC-5	4-8-8-2	8/17/29	2/8/55	25.5	To scrapper 4/18/1955.
4115	AC-5	4-8-8-2	8/15/29	1/14/54	24.4	To scrapper 6/21/1954.
4116	AC-5	4-8-8-2	8/14/29	11/10/53	24.2	SP scrapped 12/28/1953 at Sacramento.
4117	AC-5	4-8-8-2	9/6/29	1/14/54	24.4	SP scrapped 6/21/1954 at Sacramento.
4118	AC-5	4-8-8-2	8/24/29	5/7/53	23.7	SP scrapped 5/21/1953 at Sacramento.
4119	AC-5	4-8-8-2	9/5/29	5/7/53	23.7	SP scrapped 6/11/1953 at Sacramento.
4120	AC-5	4-8-8-2	9/21/29	10/6/54	25.0	To scrapper 1/3/1955.
4121	AC-5	4-8-8-2	9/23/29	5/7/53	23.6	SP scrapped 6/11/1953 at Sacramento.
4122	AC-5	4-8-8-2	9/26/29	1/14/54	24.3	SP scrapped 4/13/1954 at Sacramento.
4123	AC-5	4-8-8-2	9/25/29	11/23/53	24.2	SP scrapped 12/28/1953 at Sacramento.
4124	AC-5	4-8-8-2	10/22/29	5/7/53	23.5	SP scrapped 5/23/1953 at Sacramento.
4125	AC-5	4-8-8-2	10/23/29	5/7/53	23.5	SP scrapped 5/21/1953 at Sacramento.
4126	AC-6	4-8-8-2	7/1/30	4/20/54	23.8	SP scrapped 5/20/1954 at Sacramento.
4127	AC-6	4-8-8-2	7/11/30	2/26/54	23.6	SP scrapped 4/21/1954 at Sacramento.
4128	AC-6	4-8-8-2	8/1/30	4/14/53	22.7	SP scrapped 5/12/1953 at Sacramento.
4129	AC-6	4-8-8-2	8/2/30	5/21/54	23.8	SP scrapped 10/24/1954 at Sacramento.
4130	AC-6	4-8-8-2	8/4/30	10/6/54	24.2	To scrapper 2/4/1955.
4131	AC-6	4-8-8-2	8/5/30	9/2/54	24.1	To scrapper 11/5/1954.
4132	AC-6	4-8-8-2	8/6/30	9/2/54	24.1	To scrapper 11/15/1954.
4133	AC-6	4-8-8-2	8/21/30	9/19/55	25.1	To scrapper 1/5/1956.
4134	AC-6	4-8-8-2	8/22/30	10/6/54	24.1	To scrapper 11/24/1954.
4135	AC-6	4-8-8-2	9/6/30	5/25/55	24.7	To scrapper 6/17/1955.
4136	AC-6	4-8-8-2	9/6/30	9/19/55	25.0	To scrapper 12/5/1955.
4137	AC-6	4-8-8-2	9/4/30	4/14/53	22.6	SP scrapped 5/12/1953 at Sacramento.
4138	AC-6	4-8-8-2	9/5/30	4/14/53	22.6	SP scrapped 5/20/1953 at Sacramento.
4139	AC-6	4-8-8-2	9/17/30	6/17/54	23.8	SP scrapped 11/26/1954 at Sacramento.
4140	AC-6	4-8-8-2	10/8/30	4/5/55	24.5	To scrapper 5/23/1955.
4141	AC-6	4-8-8-2	10/16/30	10/6/54	24.0	To scrapper 2/15/1955.
4142	AC-6	4-8-8-2	10/17/30	9/2/54	23.9	SP scrapped 11/26/1954 at Sacramento.
4143	AC-6	4-8-8-2	11/15/30	9/2/54	23.8	1949 photo at Portland, OR. To scrapper 11/24/1954.
4144	AC-6	4-8-8-2	11/18/30	1/22/53	22.2	1938 photo at Dunsmuir, CA. SP scrapped 2/18/1953 at Sacramento
4145	AC-6	4-8-8-2	12/3/30	9/2/54	23.8	SP scrapped 12/30/1954 at Sacramento.

SP Cab Forward Roster Details						
Cab No.	Class	Whyte	Date In Service	Off Roster Date	Roster Years	Comments
4146	AC-6	4-8-8-2	11/26/30	9/2/54	23.8	To scrapper 11/9/1955.
4147	AC-6	4-8-8-2	12/10/30	1/22/53	22.1	SP scrapped 3/9/1953 at Sacramento. Shortest-service AC-6.
4148	AC-6	4-8-8-2	12/12/30	9/2/54	23.7	To scrapper 12/10/1954.
4149	AC-6	4-8-8-2	1/23/31	12/16/55	24.9	To scrapper 3/15/1956.
4150	AC-6	4-8-8-2	1/26/30	9/19/55	25.6	To scrapper 11/30/1955. Longest-service AC-6.
4151	AC-7	4-8-8-2	2/9/37	9/27/56	19.6	To scrapper 10/17/1956.
4152	AC-7	4-8-8-2	2/8/37	9/19/55	18.6	To scrapper 1/5/1956.
4153	AC-7	4-8-8-2	2/12/37	10/6/54	17.6	SP scrapped 12/30/1954 at Sacramento.
4154	AC-7	4-8-8-2	2/11/37	12/16/55	18.8	SP scrapped 2/13/1956 at Sacramento.
4155	AC-7	4-8-8-2	2/26/37	9/2/54	17.5	SP scrapped 11/26/1954 at Sacramento.
4156	AC-7	4-8-8-2	2/27/37	10/6/54	17.6	To scrapper 12/24/1954.
4157	AC-7	4-8-8-2	3/2/37	9/2/54	17.5	To scrapper 1/21/1955.
4158	AC-7	4-8-8-2	3/2/37	10/6/54	17.6	To scrapper 3/28/1955.
4159	AC-7	4-8-8-2	3/8/37	9/19/55	18.5	To scrapper 12/12/1955.
4160	AC-7	4-8-8-2	3/16/37	5/14/56	19.2	SP scrapped 7/30/1956 at Sacramento.
4161	AC-7	4-8-8-2	3/23/37	5/2/57	20.1	To scrapper 7/17/1957.
4162	AC-7	4-8-8-2	4/3/37	5/2/57	20.1	1947 photo at Tuscon, AZ. To scrapper 6/22/1957.
4163	AC-7	4-8-8-2	6/2/37	1/18/57	19.6	SP scrapped 2/28/1957 at Sacramento.
4164	AC-7	4-8-8-2	6/16/37	10/18/56	19.3	To scrapper 12/11/1956.
4165	AC-7	4-8-8-2	6/28/37	5/14/56	18.9	1937 photo at Kansas City, MO. To scrapper 5/31/1956.
4166	AC-7	4-8-8-2	6/30/37	9/2/54	17.2	1937 photo at Kansas City, MO. To scrapper 1/28/1955.
4167	AC-7	4-8-8-2	6/29/37	9/19/55	18.2	To scrapper 1/5/1956.
4168	AC-7	4-8-8-2	7/6/37	12/26/56	19.5	To scrapper 1/25/1957.
4169	AC-7	4-8-8-2	7/20/37	2/8/56	18.6	To scrapper 4/9/1956.
4170	AC-7	4-8-8-2	7/21/37	2/8/56	18.6	To scrapper 4/2/1956.
4171	AC-7	4-8-8-2	8/5/37	2/8/55	17.5	To scrapper 4/8/1955.
4172	AC-7	4-8-8-2	7/27/37	1/9/58	20.5	To scrapper 4/24/1959. Longest-service AC-7.
4173	AC-7	4-8-8-2	8/6/37	9/2/54	17.1	SP scrapped 7/14/1955 at Sacramento. Shortest-service AC-7.
4174	AC-7	4-8-8-2	8/17/37	2/8/55	17.5	To scrapper 4/5/1955.
4175	AC-7	4-8-8-2	9/1/37	5/2/57	19.7	To scrapper 7/17/1957.
4176	AC-7	4-8-8-2	9/21/37	9/27/56	19.0	To scrapper 11/8/1956.
4177	AC-8	4-8-8-2	8/18/39	2/8/55	15.5	To scrapper 3/3/1955.
4178	AC-8	4-8-8-2	8/25/39	9/27/56	17.1	To scrapper 10/17/1956.
4179	AC-8	4-8-8-2	8/26/39	2/8/56	16.5	To scrapper 3/15/1956.
4180	AC-8	4-8-8-2	8/28/39	10/18/56	17.1	To scrapper 12/4/1956.
4181	AC-8	4-8-8-2	9/1/39	2/7/57	17.4	To scrapper 2/28/1957.
4182	AC-8	4-8-8-2	9/2/39	9/19/55	16.0	To scrapper 12/12/1955.
4183	AC-8	4-8-8-2	9/10/39	11/15/55	16.2	To scrapper 2/8/1956.
4184	AC-8	4-8-8-2	9/13/39	9/27/56	17.0	To scrapper 10/24/1956.
4185	AC-8	4-8-8-2	9/19/39	12/28/54	15.3	To scrapper 10/24/1956.

SP Cab Forward Roster Details						
Cab No.	**Class**	**Whyte**	**Date In Service**	**Off Roster Date**	**Roster Years**	**Comments**
4186	AC-8	4-8-8-2	9/23/39	3/6/58	18.5	To scrapper 5/7/1959. Longest-service AC-8.
4187	AC-8	4-8-8-2	9/24/39	6/12/56	16.7	To scrapper 7/20/1956.
4188	AC-8	4-8-8-2	9/25/39	3/5/56	16.4	To scrapper 4/12/1956.
4189	AC-8	4-8-8-2	9/28/39	11/24/54	15.2	To scrapper 1/3/1955.
4190	AC-8	4-8-8-2	10/8/39	10/18/56	17.0	To scrapper 12/4/1956.
4191	AC-8	4-8-8-2	10/7/39	10/2/57	18.0	To scrapper 5/7/1959.
4192	AC-8	4-8-8-2	10/17/39	10/6/54	14.97	To scrapper 4/18/1955.
4193	AC-8	4-8-8-2	10/8/39	9/27/56	17.0	Burned on Santa Susana Pass (near LA), 1941 (oil feed left open while stopped for broken car coupler); to scrapper 11/6/1956.
4194	AC-8	4-8-8-2	10/18/39	10/6/54	14.97	Retired at Eugene, OR; to scrapper 2/23/1955
4195	AC-8	4-8-8-2	10/24/39	2/8/56	16.3	To scrapper 4/19/1956.
4196	AC-8	4-8-8-2	10/24/39	10/6/54	14.95	SP scrapped at Los Angeles 11-30-1954.
4197	AC-8	4-8-8-2	10/29/39	10/6/54	14.94	To scrapper 5/6/1955. Shortest-service AC-8.
4198	AC-8	4-8-8-2	10/29/39	2/8/56	16.3	To scrapper 4/3/1956.
4199	AC-8	4-8-8-2	11/3/39	6/12/56	16.6	Boiler exploded at Cooper, CA (near Salinas), 1941; to scrapper 7/20.1956.
4200	AC-8	4-8-8-2	11/7/39	4/6/56	16.4	Reused MM-2 cab number; to scrapper 5/22/1956.
4201	AC-8	4-8-8-2	11/14/39	8/9/57	17.7	Reused MM-2 cab number; to scrapper 9/18/1957.
4202	AC-8	4-8-8-2	11/14/39	8/13/56	16.8	Reused MM-2 cab number; to scrapper 10/5/1956.
4203	AC-8	4-8-8-2	11/23/39	2/8/56	16.2	Reused MM-2 cab number; to scrapper 5/1/1956.
4204	AC-8	4-8-8-2	11/26/39	2/8/56	16.2	Reused MM-2 cab number; to scrapper 5/1/1956.
4205	AC-10	4-8-8-2	2/17/42	2/7/57	15.0	Reused MM-2 cab number; to scrapper 2/28/1957.
4206	AC-10	4-8-8-2	2/21/42	1/18/57	14.9	Reused MM-2 cab number; to scrapper 2/6/1957.
4207	AC-10	4-8-8-2	3/1/42	6/12/56	14.3	Reused MM-2 cab number; to scrapper 7/26/1956.
4208	AC-10	4-8-8-2	3/2/42	9/19/55	13.6	Reused MM-2 cab number; SP scrapped 2/1/1956 at Sacramento.
4209	AC-10	4-8-8-2	3/6/42	2/17/58	16.0	Reused MM-2 cab number; to scrapper 3/23/1959.
4210	AC-10	4-8-8-2	3/9/42	12/16/55	13.8	Reused MM-2 cab number; SP scrapped 2/1/1956 at Sacramento.
4211	AC-10	4-8-8-2	3/13/42	2/7/57	14.9	Reused MM-2 cab number; to scrapper 3/7/1957.
4212	AC-10	4-8-8-2	3/22/42	3/6/58	16.0	To scrapper 5/7/1959.
4213	AC-10	4-8-8-2	3/22/42	8/13/56	14.4	To scrapper 9/14/1956.
4214	AC-10	4-8-8-2	3/28/42	9/19/55	13.5	To scrapper 9/14/1956.
4215	AC-10	4-8-8-2	4/6/42	1/18/57	14.8	To scrapper 2/1/1957.
4216	AC-10	4-8-8-2	4/8/42	5/14/56	14.1	SP scrapped 7/30/1956 at Sacramento.
4217	AC-10	4-8-8-2	4/10/42	9/27/56	14.5	To scrapper 10/24/1956.
4218	AC-10	4-8-8-2	4/15/42	3/6/58	15.9	To scrapper 3/23/1959.
4219	AC-10	4-8-8-2	4/17/42	12/16/55	13.7	SP scrapped 2/1/1956 at Sacramento.
4220	AC-10	4-8-8-2	4/21/42	9/9/57	15.4	To scrapper 4/29/1959.
4221	AC-10	4-8-8-2	4/23/42	4/5/55	13.0	SP scrapped 9/21/1955 at Sacramento.
4222	AC-10	4-8-8-2	4/27/42	2/7/57	14.8	To scrapper 2/24/1957.

SP Cab Forward Roster Details						
Cab No.	Class	Whyte	Date In Service	Off Roster Date	Roster Years	Comments
4223	AC-10	4-8-8-2	5/4/42	12/16/55	13.6	To scrapper 10/24/1956
4224	AC-10	4-8-8-2	5/4/42	5/21/58	16.0	To scrapper 10/31/1958
4225	AC-10	4-8-8-2	5/8/42	12/16/55	13.6	To scrapper 2/7/1956
4226	AC-10	4-8-8-2	5/9/42	4/5/55	12.9	SP scrapped 10/26/1955 at Sacramento
4227	AC-10	4-8-8-2	5/15/42	10/2/57	15.4	1951 photo at Los Angeles. To scrapper 4/24/1959
4228	AC-10	4-8-8-2	5/19/42	2/17/58	15.8	1947 photo at Los Angeles. To scrapper 4/24/1959
4229	AC-10	4-8-8-2	5/30/42	8/13/56	14.2	SP scrapped 10/29/1956 at Sacramento
4230	AC-10	4-8-8-2	6/3/42	12/16/55	13.5	SP scrapped 2/4/1956 at Sacramento
4231	AC-10	4-8-8-2	6/7/42	2/8/56	13.7	SP scrapped 4/20/1956 at Sacramento
4232	AC-10	4-8-8-2	6/11/42	8/13/56	14.2	To scrapper 9/11/1956
4233	AC-10	4-8-8-2	6/12/42	9/24/58	16.3	To scrapper 3/23/1959. One of last 9 cab forwards retired
4234	AC-10	4-8-8-2	6/19/42	4/5/55	12.8	SP scrapped 10/26/1955 at Sacramento.
4235	AC-10	4-8-8-2	6/20/42	10/18/56	14.3	To scrapper 11/7/1956.
4236	AC-10	4-8-8-2	7/2/42	8/9/57	15.1	To scrapper 9/18/1957.
4237	AC-10	4-8-8-2	7/9/42	5/14/56	13.9	To scrapper 6/22/1956.
4238	AC-10	4-8-8-2	7/9/42	8/13/56	14.1	To scrapper 9/11/1956.
4239	AC-10	4-8-8-2	7/12/42	4/6/56	13.7	1939 photo at El Paso, TX. To scrapper 5/17/1956.
4240	AC-10	4-8-8-2	7/13/42	1/9/58	15.5	To scrapper 5/7/1959.
4241	AC-10	4-8-8-2	7/16/42	9/24/58	16.2	To scrapper 4/24/1959. One of last 9 cab forwards retired.
4242	AC-10	4-8-8-2	7/28/42	5/21/58	15.8	To scrapper 11/3/1958.
4243	AC-10	4-8-8-2	8/6/42	9/24/58	16.1	To scrapper 8/7/1959. One of last 9 cab forwards retired.
4244	AC-10	4-8-8-2	8/19/42	5/2/57	14.7	1953 photo at Bakersfield. To scrapper 7/1/1957.
4245	AC-11	4-8-8-2	11/24/42	11/14/54	12.0	SP scrapped 1/27/55 at Sacramento.
4246	AC-11	4-8-8-2	12/1/42	1/18/57	14.1	To scrapper 2/1/57.
4247	AC-11	4-8-8-2	12/7/42	12/26/56	14.1	To scrapper 1/28/57.
4248	AC-11	4-8-8-2	12/21/42	1/18/57	14.1	To scrapper 2/1/57.
4249	AC-11	4-8-8-2	12/28/42	8/13/56	13.6	SP scrapped 10/29/56 at Sacramento.
4250	AC-11	4-8-8-2	12/30/42	2/8/56	13.1	SP scrapped 4/30/56 at Sacramento.
4251	AC-11	4-8-8-2	1/5/43	8/13/56	13.6	To scrapper 9/14/56.
4252	AC-11	4-8-8-2	1/10/43	9/24/58	15.7	To scrapper 11/22/1958. One of last 9 cab forwards retired.
4253	AC-11	4-8-8-2	1/19/43	2/8/56	13.1	1951 photo at Los Angeles. SP scrapped 4/30/56 at Sacramento.
4254	AC-11	4-8-8-2	1/19/43	4/5/55	12.2	SP scrapped 6/29/55 at Los Angeles.
4255	AC-11	4-8-8-2	1/29/43	4/5/55	12.2	SP scrapped 9/21/55 at Sacramento.
4256	AC-11	4-8-8-2	2/2/43	3/5/56	13.1	To scrapper 4/10/56.
4257	AC-11	4-8-8-2	2/5/43	9/19/55	12.6	Photo on Tehachapi Loop. To scrapper 1/25/56.
4258	AC-11	4-8-8-2	2/9/43	12/26/56	13.9	To scrapper 1/23/57.
4259	AC-11	4-8-8-2	2/13/43	2/17/58	15.0	To scrapper 4/24/59.
4260	AC-11	4-8-8-2	2/13/43	11/15/55	12.8	To scrapper 2/8/56.

SP Cab Forward Roster Details						
Cab No.	**Class**	**Whyte**	**Date In Service**	**Off Roster Date**	**Roster Years**	**Comments**
4261	AC-11	4-8-8-2	2/20/43	9/24/58	15.59	1953 photo at Los Angeles. To scrapper 4/24/59. One of last 9 cab forwards retired.
4262	AC-11	4-8-8-2	3/3/43	9/24/58	15.56	1953 photo at Los Angeles. To scrapper 7/14/59. One of last 9 cab forwards retired.
4263	AC-11	4-8-8-2	3/6/43	1/18/57	13.9	To scrapper 2/8/57.
4264	AC-11	4-8-8-2	3/9/43	5/14/56	13.2	1947 photo at Tuscon, AZ. SP scrapped 7/30/56 at Sacramento.
4265	AC-11	4-8-8-2	3/18/43	12/28/54	11.8	SP scrapped 2/21/55 at Sacramento.
4266	AC-11	4-8-8-2	3/17/43	4/5/55	12.1	SP scrapped 11/4/55 at Sacramento.
4267	AC-11	4-8-8-2	3/25/43	12/26/56	13.8	To scrapper 1/23/57.
4268	AC-11	4-8-8-2	4/1/43	4/5/55	12.0	SP scrapped 12/30/55 at Sacramento.
4269	AC-11	4-8-8-2	4/6/43	5/14/56	13.1	SP scrapped 7/30/56 at Sacramento.
4270	AC-11	4-8-8-2	4/8/43	5/14/56	13.1	To scrapper 6/22/56.
4271	AC-11	4-8-8-2	4/11/43	2/7/57	13.8	To scrapper 2/21/57.
4272	AC-11	4-8-8-2	4/18/43	9/27/56	13.4	To scrapper 10/25/56.
4273	AC-11	4-8-8-2	5/3/43	4/5/55	11.9	1952 photo at Bakersfield. SP scrapped 8/11/55 at Los Angeles.
4274	AC-11	4-8-8-2	5/9/43	2/17/58	14.8	To scrapper 3/23/59.
4275	AC-12	4-8-8-2	10/27/43	9/27/56	12.9	1947 photo at Los Angeles. To scrapper 11/8/56.
4276	AC-12	4-8-8-2	11/4/43	5/21/58	14.5	To scrapper 4/24/59.
4277	AC-12	4-8-8-2	11/8/43	4/5/56	12.4	To scrapper 5/17/1956.
4278	AC-12	4-8-8-2	11/17/43	10/2/57	13.9	1949 photo at Los Angeles. To scrapper 7/13/59.
4279	AC-12	4-8-8-2	11/28/43	4/5/55	11.4	SP scrapped 9/21/55 at Sacramento.
4280	AC-12	4-8-8-2	12/5/43	2/17/58	14.2	To scrapper 11/3/58.
4281	AC-12	4-8-8-2	12/14/43	9/24/58	14.8	To scrapper 10/31/58. One of last 9 cab forwards retired. Longest-service AC-12.
4282	AC-12	4-8-8-2	12/20/43	6/12/56	12.5	To scrapper 7/26/56.
4283	AC-12	4-8-8-2	12/26/43	9/27/56	12.8	To scrapper 10/25/56.
4284	AC-12	4-8-8-2	12/30/43	3/5/56	12.18	To scrapper 4/12/56.
4285	AC-12	4-8-8-2	1/10/44	4/6/56	12.24	To scrapper 6/22/56.
4286	AC-12	4-8-8-2	1/15/44	8/13/56	12.6	1951 photo in Oregon. SP scrapped 10/29/56 at Sacramento.
4287	AC-12	4-8-8-2	1/17/44	2/17/58	14.1	To scrapper 5/7/59.
4288	AC-12	4-8-8-2	1/17/44	4/5/55	11.22	1948 photo at Los Angeles. To scrapper 10/31/55.
4289	AC-12	4-8-8-2	1/28/44	9/24/58	14.7	1951 photo Glendale. To scrapper 3/26/59. One of last 9 cab forwards retired.
4290	AC-12	4-8-8-2	2/5/44	4/5/55	11.16	SP scrapped 11/4/55 at Sacramento.
4291	AC-12	4-8-8-2	2/13/44	4/5/55	11.14	SP scrapped 7/14/55 at Sacramento. Shortest-service AC-12.
4292	AC-12	4-8-8-2	2/21/44	9/24/58	14.6	To scrapper 11/14/58. One of last 9 cab forwards retired.
4293	AC-12	4-8-8-2	3/7/44	12/16/55	11.8	To scrapper 2/24/56
4294	AC-12	4-8-8-2	3/19/44	3/5/56	11.96	Displayed at Sacramento station, then stored until displayed in California State Railroad Museum since 1981.

Above: Co-author Vince Cipolla in the fireman's seat of AC-10 SP 4244. Richard Steinheimer Photo

Made in the USA
Lexington, KY
26 November 2019

57728306R00055